MW00810255

"The Old Testament speaks clear is evident in Heather Preston's *Between the Lines,* which addresses hope through faith from the lives of six women of the Bible. This is a powerful biblical study featuring relevant application and probing reflective questions."

—*Dr. Wayne Poplin, ThD: Professor of Old Testament Studies, Liberty University, John Rawlings School of Divinity*

"Heather writes a wonderful book about six women in the Bible to help us to put full faith in God and Him alone. You will not be disappointed in rediscovering the lives of Abigail, Ruth, Rahab, Deborah, Mary, and a woman without a name."

—*Dr. Tim Chang, PhD: Professor of Global Studies, Liberty University, John Rawlings School of Divinity*

"Author Heather Preston takes us on a deeper dive into scripture as she unpacks the Bible and stories I have read numerous times and brings fresh insight and revelation in her book *Between the Lines.* I was captivated by her sharp and insightful look into the lives of those in scripture we model ourselves after by bringing me into their world and giving me the context I need for deeper understanding. She shows the humanity of people in biblical times in a way that I can relate to in our modern day. I found myself hungry for more and captivated by each story in a way that has brought new perspective to the way I study the Bible. Her book will awaken a thirst in readers for the truth of God's Word and offers practical application of scripture in our day to day lives. This book will empower us all to pursue God to another level that will surely enhance our spiritual journey and growth. Between The Lines is a resource that brings scripture fully alive in truth and wisdom to a world that desperately needs it."

—*Irene Rollins: Author of* Reframe Your Shame, *Pastor & Speaker*

"*Between the Lines* is a beautiful fish-hook into a world that can often seem so daunting and unapproachable. The Bible is full of incredible and often lofty insight, especially when it comes to the topic of women. Heather Preston does a fantastic job of peeling back some of those intimidating layers and re-presenting truths in a way that not only illuminates God's word with simple clarity, but also helps us understand how to see ourselves in the ancient stories. We all want to be used by God, make an impact in the world and better understand our true identity in Christ. I am excited to see how this book impacts each reader to understand if God did it back then, He can surely do it again with anyone willing to take him at His powerful word! Enjoy reading... You won't regret it!"

—*Pastor Juliet Lyons, Elan Church*

"I can't think of a more timely message for a generation that perceives the Word of God as an outdated moral code to be avoided or a complex literary work to be ignored. *Between the Lines* masterfully engages the mind by not settling for the surface lessons of Scripture but by unearthing the deeper theological and cultural meaning. Heather also engages the heart through artistic storytelling, which brings these remarkable women of faith to life. Heather's passion for God's Word is palpable on every page. Reading this book will make you fall in love with God's Word all over again."

—*Senior Pastor Julie Mullins, Christ Fellowship Church*

Between the Lines

Heather Preston

Discover what you're missing
in the biblical stories
of women of faith

RIVER BIRCH PRESS

Daphne, Alabama

ISBN 978-1-956365-45-0 (print)
ISBN 978-1-956365-46-7 (e-book)

For Worldwide Distribution
Printed in the U.S.A.
River Birch Press
P.O. Box 868, Daphne, AL 36526

Table of Contents

This book is dedicated to Daddy,
the one who introduced me to Jesus.
We used to race down Dean Road.
You always won then too; but this time,
instead of a street lamp marking the finish line,
it's the Light of the World.
I know you're both smiling down.
I love you.

Preface

This book is all about faith, and though we'll look at a few characters in particular, it's everyone's story. The biblical authors paid attention to what God paid attention to—they wrote to communicate His understanding. But have you ever struggled to grasp that understanding?

I grew up in church with Sunday school, hair bows, and uncomfortable shoes. I heard the stories of the Bible my entire childhood, but it wasn't until much later in life that parts of the Bible actually made sense to me.

I knew enough to believe. I trusted God at a young age, watched Him work, and heard Him speak. But if I'm honest, my faith in God was born out of necessity during life-altering moments of pain that took me to Him. Faith opened my mind when I didn't realize it was closed.

I longed for a way to communicate the understanding that I learned through trial and tragedy. My testimony was limited, though, because simply saying that God saved my life from my own hands isn't enough. Such a statement only truly makes sense to someone who has also struggled with depression and suicidal thoughts. What about all the other people whose struggles are different? How do we connect?

Believe it or not, in the pages of some of the most boring scholarly writing I've ever read, I found it. I had to read it approximately five times for it to make sense, but I found it! I suddenly realized that the context of Scripture is everything. It was the story: the why, the how, and the very heart of God.

My mission became making this context readable. Pouring over the Bible the way the original audience would have understood it revealed a side of Scripture that I had felt but could not explain. I wanted everyone to have this experience!

I sincerely desire for everyone who reads this book to find the hope I found, which comes through faith.

Introduction

Does adversity have you discouraged, possibly questioning if God really does have a plan for you?

Though the stories of Scripture were written thousands of years ago, they are packed with tips for turning suffering into hope. The trouble is, we often miss what an ancient reader would have readily understood.

As modern readers, what would have been part of ordinary life to the original audience seems strange to us. Thus, it's easy for us to become distracted by parts that the original author never intended to emphasize. Drawing conclusions about God based on our perception of the individual characters is also easy, which creates a distance between God and us.

Like a biblical *Cliffs Notes, Between the Lines* is the brave exploration of remarkable women of faith in Scripture. Of all the books I've read in my life, the Bible is my favorite, but for me it's the studying that I enjoy. Each story is full of complex and fascinating layers. I can't get enough of Word studies and historical timelines.

This book is all about letting a reader benefit from the tools of academia like linguistic analyses, solid exegetical practices, maps, and many other tools of the trade. The goal is to go deeper and make in-depth study accessible for readers. By providing these intellectual insights in the form of storytelling, a reader can make accurate, modern-day connections and better understand an ancient culture.

Placing a reader inside the narratives of six incredible women of faith through the lens of history, language, and culture, each section focuses on an individual person. Each chapter focuses on how they maintained their faith amid great adversity.

Many of these women have been maligned and misunderstood throughout history, yet if we truly examine the Scriptures, their faith is powerfully illuminating—a testimony to a God who saw them even when society didn't. Their stories demonstrate a God who honored their faith, and through them accomplished miraculous breakthroughs for His people and for the world.

"The beginning of wisdom is this: Get wisdom, and whatever you get, get insight" (Prov. 4:7 ESV).

Since you are reading this book, I am sure that you care about gaining insight and understanding. It is the noblest pursuit to be sure, but sometimes unpacking Scripture can seem an insurmountable task.

Each of us comes to the Bible with experiences and worldviews that inherently affect our understanding of the Word. The media, our upbringing, and our cultural backgrounds all influence our perspective. When unraveling the ancient records in Scripture, certain elements that the writers would never have considered uncommon can cause readers to be diverted from the intended meaning. Because our lens is often shared by those around us, we have no one to realign us and are completely unaware of what we're missing or how our thinking has us sidetracked.

If we truly want to understand, we must be aware of our blind spots, the areas where we attempt to fill the gaps in our understanding of ancient Near Eastern life with modern, often westernized information, which inevitably leads to misunderstanding.

Sometimes we may find ourselves focusing on the New Testament out of familiarity or because it doesn't seem as foreign as the Old Testament. We shortchange our understanding by not knowing the history behind the gospel writing, for example, or Paul's epistles. Sometimes we're thrown by cultural practices that seem bizarre, actions that strike us as more overreacting (yet the authors applaud it), or by honorable characters that appear to us as marginalized. All of these scenarios can be confusing and frustrating. Written thousands of years ago, in a culture that for most is far removed from their own, the format of the Bible is intentional and sophisticated.

We know that the Bible is supposed to help us understand God, but how can we understand the Bible?

Because we can't time travel and ask the authors for explanations directly, we are reliant on data collected from various historical and archeological records for better understanding. However, most people don't have time to read scholarly theological articles or study archeological reviews to understand the significant historical events influencing what each biblical author communicates.

Grasping the sociocultural movements surrounding the pages of Scripture requires intense amounts of study. For most, that is an unrealistic goal—but that's exactly what this book makes accessible for the typical reader.

Compiling what we know from historical accounts, ancient artwork, and archeological discoveries, a steady storytelling narrative walks a reader through stories in the Bible at a depth normally only available to academics. Research only accessible to scholars, broken down and applied to each account, makes the stories come to life.

Through addressing lesser understood areas of significance like warrior or collectivist cultures, covenant laws on ritual purity, and systematic theological approaches to subjects like faith, a reader benefits from experts in their fields without the investment of a graduate degree from a school of divinity.

Furthermore, practical applications allow a reader to process the way they can utilize the truth found in the pages of Scripture in a modern setting. The Bible is filled with insights for every stage of life and every situation.

The aim of this book is to inspire readers, not just to educate them, and to allow a reader to fully experience a book that has not lost relevance, even after thousands of years. The Bible is a book of endless layers and has the answers to countless questions. If you read between the lines, I guarantee you'll be surprised by what you discover.

ABIGAIL IN THE CROSSHAIRS

Chapter 1: Know Your Worth

"He is a fool, just as his name suggests" (1 Sam. 25:25).

"You need to know this and figure out what to do" (1 Sam. 25:17). *"Then David moved down to the wilderness of Moan"* (1 Sam. 25:1).

"When the Lord has done all he has promised and has made you leader of Israel, don't let this blemish be on your record" (1 Sam. 25:30-31).

Chapter 2: Invisibility Doesn't Equal Absence

"Praise the Lord, the God of Israel, who has sent you to meet me today!" (1 Sam. 25:32)

"Bless you for keeping me from murder and from carrying out vengeance with my own hands" (1 Sam. 25:33).

"I would even be willing to become a slave" (1 Sam 25:41).

Psalms 51:10-17

Chapter 1

Know Your Worth

Some will argue that the concepts, rules, and prophecies of the Old Testament were given thousands of years ago and don't apply to people today. Or perhaps that the ancient texts from which our modern Bibles are translated were written by people, and thus contain inconsistencies and cannot be relied on. *But if this were true, how can Scripture be infallible? In other words, if the text contains errors, or it's simply that old, how can we trust what it says?*

Second Timothy tells us that all Scripture is God-breathed. Though many have sought to challenge or question how far to take the notion of infallibility (the idea that Scripture is free of any error), prophecy itself is the divine inspiration that God gives to an individual to express His Word.

Let me be clear: the Bible is divine revelation, not simply the thoughts of man. However, we are dealing with human authors who attempt to explain divine truth to a human audience. Mindsets and cultural perspectives will inherently affect how they communicate their divine Word.

Furthermore, God goes a step beyond and uses unlikely, ordinary people—not always well-educated or scholarly—to deliver His Word to the people. One such person is Abigail, and if we pay attention to her message, we catch a glimpse of a God working far outside of the social constructs of humankind.

"He is a fool, just as his name suggests" (1 Sam. 25:25).

Let's go back in time to one thousand years before Christ in a rural region of southern Israel. In the tribe of Judah, a teenage girl was married to a rich, powerful landowner named Nabal. Forty shekels were sewn into the hem of Abigail's dress, her bride price, but her mother's hands trembled with every stitch, for she knew Abigail's husband-to-be was a fool.

As soon as we're introduced to Abigail and Nabal, we are informed of their most dominant traits. I'm betting, if given the opportunity, Abigail would have objected to her own wedding. In those days, however, marriages were arranged by the parents, and often this happened in the child's infant years. Abigail would have likely had little to no say in the matter.

In 1 Samuel 25:3, Nabal is described as "surly and mean," whereas Abigail is said to be both "intelligent and beautiful." She is the only woman in the Bible described as both. Moreover, word order in the Bible is significant. Since the narrator tells us first that she is intelligent, we should consider it a key point.

The sweat ran down Nabal's arms into open scrapes as he repairs the stone wall by camp. Though Nabal's flocks of sheep were many, so too were thieves, not to mention lions and bears.

A young warrior named David had been faithfully protecting these flocks. He and his men had fended off predators, man and beast alike, and were well aware that when flocks are protected, so are finances. Though they had been sleeping in tents and building defensive walls to conceal themselves, their services had allowed Nabal to rest easily in his bed, knowing his flocks, his livelihood, were well guarded.

Therefore, after keeping watch day and night for both man and beast, David and his army had earned the right to join in the feast that came with sheering season. It's a celebration of the year's work. Considering how well the flocks have been cared for, this would be a good year for the house of Nabal! So confident was David in the service they had provided Nabal that he sent his greetings through his men.

Watching his men ride off, David senses their fatigue; his men were tired. They remain loyal to David, but most of them are not accustomed to such long watches or being exposed to the elements and estranged from their families.

Long before David had ever set foot in a palace, he had slept under the stars, caring for his father's sheep. He had been alone more than he had enjoyed comradery, but David recognized the toll that absence had taken on his men and was determined to rally morale at camp.

Because he was their commander, an attitude of honor and respect toward him was paramount. They were warriors, and he was their leader. His men needed to sense they could trust him—there could be no question as to his authority. As a man with so many servants under his command, Nabal should understand this and be well aware of the debt of provision he owes the men responsible for his protection.

In 1 Samuel 25:10 we watch Nabal's true character play out when David sends his men to request provisions. Nabal's refusal to repay David is amplified by his insulting message back to David, which no doubt is intended to humiliate the young leader.

In David's time, insults carried considerable weight when they were aimed at a warrior or a man of stature. David was one of many warriors in the ancient world who took extreme measures to protect their honor.

Warrior culture can be difficult to grasp in modern times, but this was much more than a Twitter feud! Lives hung in the balance of respect, which means that this insult called for reciprocity.

When Nabal laughs, sneering in the faces of David's soldiers, one of Abigail's servants overhears the conversation and immediately runs to tell her. Abigail is married to a foolish man and would likely become a victim because of his behavior. It is not her choice to be in the situation, but it is her choice how to act in the midst of it.

Instead of choosing to be miserable, which would be justified when one looks at the character of Nabal, Abigail chooses to hold to the hope only found in faith. Furthermore, she chooses to act.

Her actions are about to set in motion events that would save lives and alter history.

"Not again!" Abigail's servant mutters through gritted teeth. Locking up the grain silo behind him at record pace, he set off to find her.

If the offense wasn't so abhorrent, the servant would merely be annoyed, which was typical around Nabal. However, offending David after he and his army had protected them all this time was beyond stupidity.

But it was no use trying to reason with Nabal. He was his namesake—a fool. Fortunately, the servant also knew who would respond to reason, and as fast as he could, he raced to Abigail.

Panting and out of breath, he relays Nabal's crude remarks, growing more and more frustrated. Finally, he says, "Think it over and tell us what to do, for we will surely die if we don't act quickly!"

This is not the first time Abigail had avoided imminent disaster caused by her brute of a husband. Though Nabal views her as no more than property, the servants had come to depend on Abigail, and this time the stakes are higher than ever. In retaliation to Nabal's offense, David's entire army is on their way to kill every member of Nabal's family, including the servants. It would make a statement to both David's men, and any neighboring tribe, that David is the anointed king who deserved respect.

As a woman of her position in society, becoming bitter would have been easy for Abigail. She was essentially property. The quality of life in the ancient world depended on owning land, which required being a man or being married to one. Abigail was caught in the crosshairs of one very foolish man, who made daily life miserable, and another whose temper was leading him into a murderous mistake. Clearly the servant in verse 17 knew whom to turn to!

The conversation between Abigail and the servant shows no hesitation on behalf of either. They spoke freely, and the servant has total confidence that Abigail will know how to proceed, which she "wasted no time" doing (1 Sam. 25:18). She also did not ask permission. Verse 19 states clearly, "She did not tell her husband." This is a woman with a plan, who needs no prompting to do what is right.

Abigail was likely riding toward her own death. David might not listen to her, providing she even had the opportunity to reason with him. Nonetheless, she began praying and practicing what she would say as she rode toward his army.

Abigail tried to imagine herself in his shoes. David was on the run, betrayed by his own mentor, living like an outlaw. His men were depending on him, but they're also quite likely questioning his anointing and missing home.

Abigail knew that she must make her appeal in such a way that he would want to listen. Before Abigail could reach David and his armies, we witness David becoming even more enraged. Have you ever relived an offense in your mind and made yourself more upset, which in turn only made the situation worse? When Abigail makes her case to David, that's his headspace.

Even her posture is significant. Before ever speaking and asking David to spare the lives of her family, Abigail bowed to the ground. She has no doubt been thinking through her speech the entire way. Leaders instinctively identify faults in others, but good leaders don't solely point them out. They help their followers avoid the pitfalls of their weaknesses. Abigail is about to help David avoid his.

Consider Abigail's speech, which is the longest of any woman in the Bible. Her words in 1 Samuel 25:24–31 are elegant, well-spoken, and express a shared vision. Abigail began by apologizing for a situation she had no control over but that had offended David. She hadn't committed the offense, but by expressing shared outrage, she earned the right to continue speaking.

She acknowledged David's desire for vengeance but wisely reminded him that he had a higher calling. Abigail showed no ambiguity regarding his anointing as king, despite his circumstances at the time, and used this to reason with him. In verse 30 she said to David that after the Lord had done all He promised and made him leader of Israel, he shouldn't let this be a blemish on his record. In other words, he should think ahead! David's response speaks of her wisdom and his arguably deepest flaw—a tendency to wage war. In verse 33 he says to her, "Thank God for your good sense! Bless you for keeping me from murder."

"Good sense" can also mean "advice or judgment." David was not immune to Abigail's beauty, but here he applauds her counsel and intelligence. Abigail could have let her circumstances define her. She could have let being married to a fool be her legacy. Instead, she flipped the script and claimed the identity God spoke over her: a woman of great intelligence and beauty, a woman of wisdom who would save her people.

Praise the Lord, the God of Israel, who has sent you to meet me today!" (1 Sam. 25:32)

Abigail was like a vision riding toward David. The hem of her skirt floated around her as the evening breeze tousled the hair escaping her tichel, a headscarf carefully knotted at the base of her pretty head. Her effortless dismount was like a dance, but before David could utter a word, this enchanting figure bowed low to the ground, her expensively dyed garments pressing into the rocky soil.

David dared not glance at his men, for surely the king should have the first word. Instead, Abigail was the one who spoke, and the words that poured forth from her pouted lips were as eloquent as they were discerning.

Before moving forward in our story, I want to take a closer look at Abigail's appeal. After thirteen years of marriage, I can credit a significant percentage of our arguments to wanting to be heard. I wasn't necessarily mad at *what* my husband said. It was *the way* he said it! Sound familiar?

There's nothing quite like our need as humans to feel seen and heard. Abigail clearly understood this, and she mentioned a number of things past, present, and future that significantly could alter David's perspective on the confrontation. Like a good lawyer, she never lost sight of her objective.

Throughout her petition, Abigail placed the focus on the providential hand of their mutual God. Her mention of "stones shot from a sling" was an allusion to Goliath and the victory God gave Israel through the hero, David. First Samuel 25:29 states, "Even though you are chased by those who seek to kill you, your life is safe in the care of the Lord your God." Here Abigail seemed to simultaneously praise David's victorious stature while also reminding him where that victory originated.

Why was an anointed king on the run for his life in the first place? This very anointing was what enraged his former mentor and current king, Saul. Saul had turned from God, and the prophet Samuel had made it clear that because he did, Saul could no longer be king of Israel. In 1 Samuel 15, the prophet tells him, "So because you have rejected the command of the Lord, he has rejected you as king."

Saul is a clear example of how our response to God matters to Him and impacts how He responds to us. At this point, like an angry child who doesn't get what he wants, Saul was gunning for David.

Abigail recognized this and even prophesied that David will have a "lasting dynasty," which would have taken considerable faith to believe in considering his predicament as a fugitive. Abigail was uniquely positioned to understand David's feelings of injustice, of being dismissed and disrespected. She was, after all, married to a man who was characterized as crude and mean.

But Nabal's biblical description implies far more than him being an unpleasant roommate. You see, it's very unlikely Nabal's parents named him "fool." In fact, the word fool in Hebrew was traditionally a euphemism for serious sin, the kind of sin that destroys or endangers tribal or familial relationships. It typically concerned sexual assault. Examples include the rape of Dinah (Gen. 34:7) and the rape of Tamar (2 Sam. 13:12).

While we are not told explicitly of Nabal's past grievances, because the author, perhaps even the townsfolk, used this name, we can infer a considerable weight to the severity of his character flaws. Knowing this only adds to the courage of Abigail's obedience to God.

Furthermore, Abigail clearly read between the lines of Nabal's rebuff to David. His arrogant jest of "Who is this fellow, David?" isn't a profession of ignorance but an outright rejection of David's request, which goes against Israeli laws of provision for sojourners.

Nabal knew who David was, the son of Jesse. We can almost hear the sarcastic tone of his reply in 1 Samuel 25:10 when he says, "There are many servants today who are breaking away from their masters." He was laughing at David, mocking him behind his back to his army. David was being deprived of his rightful status as king and the lawful provisions owed to him and his soldiers.

Abigail did not dismiss this. She acknowledged Nabal's desire for vengeance, even though she clearly saw it as the wrong course of action. Although Abigail empathized with Nabal's anger, she advised David against retaliation. She lived out this conviction in her life and did not let her marriage to Nabal corrupt her character. One can't help but get a sense of Abigail's hope for her future as she humbly requests, "Remember me, your servant." A future was about to unfold in dramatic fashion.

Reflection

1. What are some circumstances in your life that you are struggling with?

2. How are you choosing to act in your situation?

3. Do your actions reflect your character?

4. The name Abigail means "joy of her father." Although we may have serious doubts about her earthly father after marrying her to Nabal, consider how this name characterizes her relationship with her heavenly Father.

5. Do you find it hard to be humble when you know you're right?

6. How might you apply Abigail's tactics those who disagree with you? How might you show your understanding of their situation?

7. What are offenses in your life that you struggle to let go of?

8. How might your response to those offenses represent your identity in Christ?

Chapter 2

Invisibility Doesn't Equal Absence

It seemed ages since the day Samuel anointed David and declared him God's chosen king. The years David spent under Saul's mentorship felt like a lifetime ago. His family, his best friend, Jonathan, and his wife Michal were all part of distant yet painful memories.

The anger within him burned as he drew nearer to Nabal's home, but the sadness remained a hollow ache. In the palace, it was easy to believe that he was the anointed one. After all, he had frequently occupied the king's throne room, was best friends with prince Jonathan, and had even married the king's daughter. His life had the impression of everything coming together for David.

But now, his ideal life seemed as if it had all been a dream, for he was once again a shepherd. He was no longer well-groomed or robed in purple. Calloused and ruddy, darkened by the sun, wet with dew every morning, and smelling of livestock, David was hardly the picture of royalty.

Had God forgotten?

Despite David currently being in a real-life Hunger Games, Abigail still says "when" not "if" regarding the Lord making him king. She shows no doubt regarding David's future. Abigail trusts that God is orchestrating a plan and working all things for good.

Now was David's turn to speak. David clearly sees Abigail as "sent by God." From the servant's reaction, going and requesting the counsel of Abigail, we have already witnessed much about Abigail's character. David and his servant knew who would save them from retaliation.

In verse 32 David recognized Abigail's wisdom, blessed her, and acknowledged what she has done for him. She had presented her counsel flawlessly and transfixed the future king.

Mesmerized, the king descends from his horse. He's taller than he first appeared and carries himself like a trained fighter. Yet, crouching next to her, girded with a sword and equipped for battle, he cannot help but feel vulnerable. Her humility exists in tandem with the countenance befitting a queen.

It has been a long time since anyone has had such an effect on him. David's hand trembles slightly as he lifts her face to look at him. As their eyes lock, the moment lingers. David thanks her, but he wishes to say far more to her as he sends her home in peace.

Other than the servants assisting her and David's army, no one knows what Abigail has been doing this evening, and she knew no one would be paying attention to her with feast preparations underway.

Sheering season was a raucous time for Nabal. Everything was served in excess, especially the wine. Tonight would be no exception. Without Abigail interceding, the potential damage Nabal could do that night weighed heavily on her shoulders.

Remember how Abigail "didn't tell her husband what she was doing" (1 Sam. 25:19)? Although she was brilliantly successful in brokering peace, we don't see an immediate reversal for Abigail. In fact, she didn't get so much as a thank you. Instead, when she arrived home that evening, her husband was throwing a party and apparently very drunk.

What we can often miss as we judge Nabal's behavior is that

he wasn't just the villain of this story. He's the picture of a sinner who repeatedly rejects God without regard to the consequences. Nabal could have easily invited David to his feast and was most certainly wealthy enough to feed him and his entire army. Instead, he endangered his family and all those with him, pretending that all was well. Likewise, when we ignore caution in God's Word, we invite the consequences.

Picking up the array of clothing Nabal had chosen to remove during tonight's festivities, Abigail does not bother greeting her inebriated husband. She watches as he knocks over his mostly empty glass and shouts insults at a neighbor, none of which makes any sense. Shaking her head, Abigail decides to wait until morning to recount her day's activities.

Once again, Abigail refused to stoop to Nabal's level. Knowing it wouldn't do any good to say anything to him in his condition, she doesn't even inform him that she saved his life, and the entire family, until morning. What most of us wouldn't see coming is his reaction.

Abigail has been up for hours before Nabal stumbles into the daylight. While he was still rubbing his eyes and nursing a hangover, Abigail waits. Though he had spent much time that morning cursing and muttering that he couldn't remember what happened the night before, when she finally tells him of her encounter with David, Nabal is silent.

Suddenly and violently, Nabal grabs at his chest. Then like a stone, he hits the floor. Ten days later, the Lord strikes Nabal, and he dies.

The Bible has a lot to say about choosing to love over being bitter. In fact, it has a lot to say about the heart in general. The kind of self-control Abigail exhibited shows how well she had resisted bitterness. Proverbs 4:23 says, "Above all else, guard your heart, for everything you do flows from it." The ancient Hebrew authors saw a person's heart as the epicenter of their intellectual and emotional capacities from where they would make choices. It should come as no surprise, then, that prior to this statement, the biblical author is repeatedly urging, "Get wisdom."

Abigail lived out this concept, upholding the law and remaining faithful to God. Nabal hardened his heart and refused to obey the prophet Zechariah, who spoke the word of God to the people, saying, "Act with love and compassion toward one another . . . the sojourner and the poor" (Zech. 7:9). Therefore, when Abigail told him of her diplomatic success, Nabal was not pleased. In fact, when Abigail informed him of her actions the day before, he had a heart attack.

First Samuel 25:37 says that Nabal became "like a stone." One can't help but think of Abigail's prophecy that David's enemies will "disappear like stones." But the Bible is clear: Abigail is not the cause of Nabal's death. Not even the shock of her news is the cause of his death. Vengeance is carried out by God. Verse 38 says, "The Lord struck Nabal, and he died."

When we consider how concerned Abigail was for David not to have unnecessary blood on his hands and examine her actions throughout this chapter, we glimpse an even fuller picture of the depth of her faith. She exhibited total confidence that the Lord would avenge those who are mistreated and never allowed herself to be swayed by the actions of those around her. As we will see, God most certainly did avenge her.

David could not get Abigail out of his mind. Only a few days had passed, and she was still married to Nabal, but he couldn't stop thinking about her. One night as he cleaned some wild game with his men around a fire, he glanced at the blood on his hands and recalled Abigail's words: "The Lord has restrained you from bloodguilt . . . let your enemies and those who seek to harm you be like Nabal."

David knew she meant that the Lord would avenge him, but how? When? Or was he simply holding out hope that Abigail would come back into his life?

After a couple weeks had passed, David felt he would have to let her go. He and his men needed to move on to Ziph. Saul and his armies would likely have tracked them by now, and besides, after the confrontation with Nabal, they clearly were not welcome here.

But even as David contemplated their next move, some of his scouts rode in with word of Nabal's death. David wasted no time. Though he could not leave his post, he carefully composed verses that his scouts were under strict orders to recite verbatim. As a renowned songwriter, he felt the pressure of those verses. But he also knew how badly he needed her, for after all, "A woman of wisdom, who can find?" (Prov. 31:10)

Without doubt, David saw in Abigail more than a pretty face to adorn his future palace. David continually struggled with a tendency toward violence, and this failing is one that Abigail circumvents. David clearly recognized this, rightfully blessing her.

After Abigail's death and without her counsel, David tendency toward violence was the reason 1 Chronicles gives for him not being able to rebuild God's temple. Think of that—the greatest king Israel will ever know was unable to build God's temple because of a violent streak. Instead, God chose his son Solomon to build the temple, a man who was renowned for his wisdom. Remind you of anyone?

Before we get there, let's look at the way that the narrator set up this pivotal moment in David and Abigail's story. The narrator neither endorsed nor objected to David's murderous intentions.

Abigail did both. She put herself in his shoes and acknowledges the offense against him, the lack of honor showed him, the unfair situation before him. Far too often, we forget to do this when we object to the actions of others. Without first acknowledging David's pain, she would have had no right to continue speaking. It is highly unlikely that he would have listened to her without her humble approach, and even less likely he would have offered her a king's blessing.

Of the women in his life, David's time with Abigail is depicted as his best. His most noble traits are visible when she is in the picture. In fact, in the years after she fades from view, David begins to regress. Abigail most certainly embodied the truth of Proverbs 27:17 (ESV) which states, "Iron sharpens iron, and one man sharpens another." Without a doubt, Abigail "sharpened" David.

"I would even be willing to become a slave" (1 Sam. 25:41).

Before David's men reached her, Abigail knew why they were there. She too had felt a connection, though for Abigail, David was a long-awaited answer to prayer. Abigail had only ever wanted to serve God and help her people. The servants who recognized her wisdom had also benefitted from the purity of her heart and her willingness to intercede wherever an offense had been committed, regardless of where the blame should lie.

Though she believes David would eventually be king, she is hardly "trading up." Abigail remains a humble agent of the Lord as she accepts the life of a fugitive.

Abigail would legally inherit a considerable fortune upon her husband's death, yet she declares that she would willingly become a slave in service to the anointed king, "washing his servant's feet." Humility was always at the core of Abigail's approach and the core of how she lived her life.

Too often we equate humility with low self-esteem, when in

fact the two are nowhere near compatible. In fact, often those who are most prideful are simply overcompensating for low self-esteem.

Humility is a condition of the heart. Remember David struggling after Abigail faded from the picture? He writes a prayer in Psalms 51:10 (ESV) asking God to, "Create in me a clean heart . . . and renew a right spirit in me." What a powerful appeal we might all consider praying.

Humility isn't about putting oneself down but rather lifting God up. It's about being so aware of the greatness of God that you would say with Abigail, "I would even be willing to become a slave!" The Bible tells us that "The Lord lifts up the humble" (Ps.147:6). Therefore, if we believe the Scriptures, we should gladly lay aside our pride.

The Bible says we are:

His Masterpiece: "For we are the product of His hand, heaven's poetry etched on lives, created in the Anointed, Jesus, to accomplish the good works God arranged long ago" (Eph. 2:10).

Called by Name: "See, you have nothing to fear. I, who made you, will take you back. I have chosen you, named you as My own" (Isa. 43:1).

Chosen: "Since you are all set apart by God, made holy and dearly loved, clothe yourselves with a holy way of life: compassion, kindness, humility, gentleness, and patience" (Col. 3:12).

Yet all of this is ultimately meaningless if we don't choose to live in submission to His plan, for God will never force us to trust or love Him. The choice is ours; we can either live in His purpose as Abigail did, or let our own selfishness be our downfall like Nabal did and die as a fool.

Consider Abigail, who was born into a society where her marriage was arranged when she was a child. She was likely a bride before her sixteenth birthday. This was her role, her defining identity. Clearly the servants recognized her wisdom, but it's unlikely many around her would have lauded this quality.

I can vividly remember being asked as soon as I was engaged (even before) if I wanted children. In Abigail's day this would not have been a question but rather the expectation. Who but God could have imagined this girl saving His anointed from sin and bearing royal heirs, rather than sons of a "fool"?

Abigail's perspective and approach to David was undoubtedly influenced by her life experiences. Perhaps having to deal with Nabal sharpened her negotiation skills. However, that doesn't change the fact that her message was divinely inspired.

In the same way that a chauvinistic society didn't eliminate Abigail from God's plan, the infallibility of Scripture—or reliability, for that matter—does not exclude the use of human authors. In fact, God seems particularly fond of using the unlikely candidates, and we should be thankful that God uses us to accomplish His purposes.

However, I think infallibility is a bit of a difficult concept for a modern audience because so much of our news and information is based on opinion. We are bombarded by a seemingly endless feed of information but nothing that truly makes us think, which is harmful to our understanding of the supernatural. God can and does inspire divine messages for His people, but if we are too busy listening to opinions that mirror our own, we are apt to miss it.

Although our lives may look remarkably different from the characters we read about in Scripture, ultimately the Bible is the story of God redeeming His creation. The Bible isn't the story of Abigail or David—it's all about God. When we get caught up in attempting to explain these "errors," we very often forget about the metanarrative of Scripture and fail to consider the author's true purpose in writing.

Reflection

1. Are there areas of your life that you struggle to surrender to God?

2. We've all heard it said we are the sum of our closest friends, but do you always ensure that your closest friends bring out your best?

3. What kind of friend are you? Do you bring out the best in your friends?

4. Do you struggle to remain faithful when your actions go unnoticed?

5. Is your idea of fairness shaped more by society or the Bible?

6. How do you make sure your motives honor God?

7. Physical conditions in the Bible often represent moral states. The "hardening of the heart" is something we see more than once in Scripture. Consider Pharoah (Ex. 7:13, 22; 8:32; 9:35). He hardened his heart and refused to listen to God, despite numerous miracles. Both Pharoah and Nabal were wealthy men who leveraged their position at the expense of others. Abigail's countenance is marked by humility but Nabal's by pride. Consider this as you read Proverbs 29:23.

8. When listening to a preacher or teacher, do you find it hard to get past someone's physical or cultural differences? Do you find that most evangelists you listen to or follow look and sound like you? Challenge yourself to expand your borders. God's people come from all corners of the globe.

RUTH, THE FOREIGNER

Chapter 3: Going Against Social Norms

Ruth 1

"But on the way, Naomi said to her two daughters-in-law, "Go back" (Ruth 1:8).

"Don't ask me to leave you and turn back. Wherever you go, I will go; wherever you live, I will live. Your people will be my people, and your God will be my God" (Ruth 1:16).

Ruth 2

"May the LORD, the God of Israel, under whose wings you have come to take refuge, reward you fully for what you have done" (Ruth 2:12).

Chapter 4: Tuning Out the Naysayers

Ruth 3–5

"Who are you?" he asked. "I am your servant Ruth," she replied. "Spread the corner of your covering over me, for you are my family redeemer" (Ruth 3:9).

"For he is the son of your daughter-in-law who loves you and has been better to you than seven sons!" (Ruth 4:15).

"And they named him Obed, He became the father of Jess and the grandfather of David" (Ruth 4:17).

Chapter 3

Going Against Social Norms

Every year just before Easter, usually on Good Friday, Christians all over the world listen to a message about what happened the day Christ was crucified. Every year, we talk about the temple veil, which separated man from the Holy of Holies and the very presence of God, being torn in half and Jesus making a way for everyone to go directly to Him.

However thrilling this is for those of us who have accepted Christ, for the Jews at the time, this would have been terrifying. The temple veil signified the Old Covenant, and their practices and customs pertaining to the temple were their way—their only way—of atoning for sin and remaining loyal to God.

Therefore, even those Jews who followed Jesus would have been confused and likely wondering if evil had triumphed, asking themselves what it all meant.

The Gospel of Matthew's inclusion of two "outsiders" in Jesus' direct genealogical line is very intentional. Ruth was a Moabite and Rahab a Canaanite, but both had been grafted into the lineage of the Messiah by faith.

The writers of the New Testament are celebrating what before Christ was unthinkable—a family of God that united all through faith in one Savior. In Hebrews, Paul gives an account of the legendary characters of the Bible and distinguishes all of them by their faith. From Abraham to Rahab, he makes clear that their defining trait wasn't their race or origin but their allegiance to

God. He states that they did not cling to the home they knew of on earth: "They desire a better country, that is, a heavenly one. Therefore God is not ashamed to be called their God, for he has prepared them a city."

In the same way Abraham left his home country to follow God, so too these women forsook everything they knew, declaring faith in the one true God. They declared allegiance to a kingdom beyond the natural, and in doing so, their inheritance became supernatural. Their self-abandonment preserved them in the very canon of Scripture.

"But on the way, Naomi said to her two daughters-in-law, 'Go back'" (Ruth 1:8).

Go back to roughly thirteen hundred years before Christ, somewhere between Saudi Arabia and Ethiopia. A Jewish woman was pleading with her Moabite daughters-in-law to leave her. She had been living in the forbidden land of Moab, where she and her husband had made a life together, and where her sons had met and married their wives. It's also where they died.

Her plea was not a matter of love-loss. Rather, Naomi understands the cruelty of life for a woman without a husband or sons. Her fate would now utterly depend on the pity of others. She had a better chance of finding compassion in Bethlehem, but Orpah and Ruth were too young to give up on their future, and their families were there in Moab.

Besides, the faith they had come to learn from Naomi was shaken, possibly gone. How could God have let this happen to her?

The book of Ruth starts off pretty bleak. Naomi and her two daughters-in-law have recently lost everything. By modern standards this is a devastating loss. In ancient times, these three women were now also homeless and reliant on charity from others.

On top of this, Naomi announced her husband's death. Elimelech is not a name we hear today, but it translates to "my God is king." When Naomi announced his death and the loss of her two sons, her despair is three-fold. In addition to living in a foreign land, she was then entirely estranged from God's chosen people. She regarded her tragedies as God turning against her, which is why her sense of loss was not only physical but spiritual. Naomi had lost her future and her faith.

Knowing this, it is not surprising when Naomi told Ruth and Orpah to go back home and find new husbands. Since neither Orpah nor Ruth have children, we can safely assume they are still quite young. Logically, Naomi's advice made sense; if they returned to their parents, surely they could start families of their own.

But Moab wasn't Naomi's home. She and her husband had left their Israelite community when Bethlehem experienced famine. There we find the tables had turned, and Moab was in famine.

The situation became even more complicated regarding the relationship between these two lands. Moab, and specifically the women of Moab, were seen as pagan temptresses who led the Israeli men away from their faith and destroyed the Israelite's cultural identity as God's chosen people. Naomi's best option was to return to Bethlehem and hope for someone to take pity on her, but she had reason to not want Ruth to accompany her.

Ruth knew the history. She and her late husband, Mahlon, once talked about the storied past between the Moabites and the Israelites. But Ruth wasn't like most Moabite women. In fact, she'd always felt as a bit of a foreigner in her land. Though she had been raised to believe in many gods, it wasn't until she heard of Yahweh that she truly felt faith stirring within her. Surely this was the true God.

Ruth also knew the cost of leaving Moab. She was leaving

behind friends and family, everything she knew, and would not be welcome in Bethlehem. Surely no Israeli man would want a Moabite bride. In fact, as a young woman in a strange land, she would easily become prey, for who would even defend such a woman? Was it worth the risk?

Ruth was a foreigner and a Moabite. Along with the afore-mentioned qualities, Moab is a land that can trace its heritage to incest (Gen. 19:3–37). The Israelites specifically blamed the women of Moab for an era in which, "The Lord's anger burned against them [Israel]" (Num. 25:1–3). The original audience for the book of Ruth would have been incredibly skeptical about the main character of the story.

When Ruth heard Naomi say, "Go back!" she was fully aware of the complicated dynamic at work. She knew that she was young and capable of rebuilding a life, had family who would shelter her, and would likely be no more welcome in Bethlehem than she was with Naomi at that moment. But Ruth chose to defy social norms and made a declaration of faith, saying, "Your people will be my people, and your God will be my God" (Ruth 1:16).

While Naomi continued to be overwhelmed by circumstances, Ruth chose to be controlled by her faith. And it is for this faith that she became part of a divine narrative, one that would make a way for future generations!

The whispers were not as quiet as they apparently thought. It sounded like hissing as Ruth and Naomi made their way through the city gate. The stares were visceral, some people were even pointing.

"Is this Naomi?" one woman cried in disbelief.

Naomi could bear it no more. "Call me Mara!" she said, weeping bitterly. "The Highest One has brought disaster on me."

Ruth attempted to comfort her, which brought even more questions. Had God judged Naomi for keeping company with the likes of Ruth? With Moabites?

When we first encountered Naomi, it was a fairly abrupt introduction. She was attempting to rid herself of her daughters-in-law and denounce her faith. Have you ever taken a friend's words to heart, only to realize that they were going through something, and you were the convenient place to vent? Maybe they negatively criticized you or spoke too harshly, and it made you doubt yourself or your relationship with them? It's a similar moment when we first meet Naomi.

As described earlier, she had recently lost both of her sons and her husband. Because they had moved to a foreign land, she was entirely estranged from God's chosen people; her sense of loss was bone deep. It was her entire identity.

Naomi continues to weep aloud. Ruth guides her gently to a bench close by, afraid that in her hysterics she might fall if she doesn't sit down. Ruth tries to look around for some idea of what to do or where they might go, but it proves pointless without Naomi. Bethlehem is as different from Moab as she had always imagined. Ruth is unsure where they could spend the night, let alone where they might find food.

Tired and hungry, Ruth's feet are badly blistered from their journey and her skin the shade of midnight from days spent traveling in the hot sun. Part of her wants to crack, to question her decision to come. Part of her wants to curl up next to Naomi and let the gravity of her situation cripple her.

While avoiding the anxious stares of strangers, she watches as the evening breeze gently rocks the stalks of barley ready for harvest. Somehow it is comforting. Ruth lets her mind wander, and for a moment, the bitter wailing of her mother-in-law fades.

For a moment, Ruth feels comforted.

For Naomi to announce her forlorn state to her two daughters-in-law, who are both from Moab, would be like exposing a wound. We understand immediately that her return to Bethlehem would not be dignified. Also, her departure from Bethlehem was during a season of lack. Bethlehem means "House of Bread," but when Naomi and her late husband left, the land was anything but filled with bread. Now, as she returned alone and empty-handed, Bethlehem was once again plentiful.

Can you picture her friend's faces seeing her limp back home? Naomi had gone looking for "better" and lost everything. Obviously, she would prefer as few witnesses to her shame as possible. But this is where Naomi's emotions trump her faith.

Faith should never be relegated to a feeling. Though Naomi had experienced an overwhelming amount of tragedy, and her feelings of despair are quite justified, her response to God in those circumstances was not one of faith but emotion.

Ruth, on the other hand, who has also lost her husband and could easily allow her emotions to drive her back to the arms of family and familiarity, stepped out in faith. In one of the most famous verses of the Bible, Ruth told Naomi, "Don't ask me to leave you and turn back. Wherever you go, I will go; wherever you live, I will live. Your people will be my people, and your God will be my God" (Ruth 1:16).

When hard times hit, and we are assured by Scripture they will, our response should be one that turns our attention to God. Jesus tells us in John 16:33, "In the world you will have tribulation. But take heart; I have overcome the world."

In this way, the book of Ruth reminds us that faith keeps us in the providential hand of God. Faith connects us to the unchanging One in the midst of turmoil. Ruth understood this, and her faith altered the course of her life. She stepped from destitution to destiny.

"What have I done to deserve such kindness?" she asked. "I am only a foreigner" (Ruth 2:10).

As if the task of collecting other's scraps weren't humbling enough, she could feel the hot, disapproving stares from those around her. Ruth had sought Naomi's advice on which field would be safest, but she knew to watch her back. She had already caught the eye of more than one of the young men working, and their sneers made her nervous.

You may have noticed or even been distracted by the constant reference to Ruth as a "foreigner" or a "Moabite." This is not a repetitious error the author made. We're supposed to notice it to see what Ruth was enduring. This was no vacation.

At the beginning of chapter two, she asks Naomi if she can "pick up the stalks of grain left behind by anyone who is kind enough to let me do it." How glamorous, right? She couldn't have been in a more pitiful station in the ancient world. Like collecting soda cans in modern times, she was collecting scraps out of a stranger's field to feed herself and her mother-in-law.

Yet, Ruth proceeded to live out her faith. When we trust God and live out our faith, even silently like Ruth, it gets noticed. In chapter 2, verse 5, Boaz inquired about Ruth.

She had clearly already been noticed by Boaz's overseer, for he was able to tell Boaz her name, foreign status, and details of how hard she has worked with only a short rest. As he asked about Ruth, we can't help but wonder about Boaz.

His robes are far too expensive for a field laborer, and he carries himself like a man who knows his authority. It was immediately obvious that this was his field. For a moment, Ruth trembles. Is he offended by her presence? Would he take the grain she had gleaned thus far and send her back to Naomi empty-handed? Just as she feels her hope evaporating, he greets her with an unexpectedly disarming smile.

Only a few verses in, and the reader is already attracted to Boaz's generous and charismatic nature. He is the biblical Romeo. His name attaches further importance to his role, as it is the Hebrew word for "guardian-redeemer." The reference being made is both specific in nature as well as metaphorical.

The book of Leviticus details Israeli law regarding a "kinsman redeemer," and if a relative was forced to sell their land due to poverty, a close relative or "kinsman" could legally buy it back to "redeem" their family. Such instances legally provided for widows and orphans, those would otherwise have nowhere to go, with no other option in the ancient world.

Now, it would be easy to equate Boaz to a Prince Charming saving the day, as Ruth gets married, lives happily ever after, etc. But that interpretation would entirely miss the point. Boaz metaphorically represents God's plan to rescue all nations, to rescue all of us.

You see, the book of Ruth is significantly tied to the land. Abraham (ancestor of Boaz) and Lot (ancestor of Ruth) separated because Lot was enticed by the land to the east (Genesis 13:10), which eventually led to a tragic end. Naomi and Elimelech left Bethlehem, the land from which they could claim an inheritance, to find greater wealth to the east. Naomi is now without either land or wealth. In fact, she doesn't even have an heir to be remembered by. Ruth is the unlikely story of a family's reunification.

Abraham's offspring are represented by Bethlehem and Lot's by the land of Moab. Lot was seduced by prosperity and strayed from God. In contrast, Ruth exemplifies love and faithfulness and was subsequently blessed beyond what she could have possibly imagined.

Ruth courageously represented the people God wants to bring back to Himself, which is why she appeared centuries later in the New Testament as a parallel example of God's overall plan for creation.

A larger story was at work than Ruth's life turning out well. She was about to find herself playing a critical role in the redemption of the world because she had faith.

Reflection

1. How many times in life have you felt as if you were working beneath your calling?

2. Do you find it hard to stay faithful when you don't see immediate results?

3. Have you ever experienced a loss that made you question what you believe?

4. Was your response like Naomi's or Ruth's?

5. What are some areas where you've faced opposition or felt overwhelmed by your circumstances?

6. When Ruth boldly proclaims her allegiance to Naomi and Naomi's God, she is actually making an oath. In Ruth 1:17 she in fact implicates herself by vowing that nothing "but death separate us." This is a definite factor in Naomi's relenting. Ruth's vow essentially binds them together. Making such a promise takes tremendous courage.

7. What's an area in your life where you feel challenged to step out in faith?

Chapter 4

Tuning Out the Naysayers

At mealtime, Ruth looks around for somewhere to rest where she will not intrude. The workers clearly have their groups, and each eagerly begins to talk and laugh. Once again, she feels her isolated status and immediately wants to hide.

Just then, to her surprise, Boaz invites her to his table. Suddenly conscious of her appearance, Ruth attempts to wipe the sweat from her brow, only to smear dusty sand across her face. Seeing her discomfort, Boaz once again flashes his infectious smile, and at once she feels herself at ease, while also entirely self-aware.

His table is laden with bread, pesto, hummus, and dried fruits. A bowl of olives tantalizes Ruth, the scent of the spices and wine wafting toward her. Despite the sumptuous food laid out before her, Ruth imagines sitting at his table would be immensely uncomfortable—full of all the "new girl" questions that would subsequently funnel into the rumor mill.

But she is pleasantly surprised when Boaz, instead of interrogating her on her past, makes conversation about the present. He makes a point of commenting on the kindness she has shown Naomi. He even offers a blessing, and loudly enough for others to hear, says, "May the LORD, the God of Israel, under whose wings you have come to take refuge, reward you fully for what you have done" (Ruth 2:12).

Then, as though he senses her avoidance of the spotlight, he says, "Here, dip your bread in this!" During the rest of the meal, Boaz makes easy conversation with everyone at the table and encourages her to sample everything until she is so full she can eat no more.

What stands out to Ruth about Boaz was not his status or his hospitality, though it is exceptionally gracious, but he has an air about him of confidence. It isn't arrogance but instead a kind of knowing that immediately invites one to trust him.

The title of "kinsman-redeemer" is a translation of the Hebrew word *go'el*. The legal term is used twelve times in the Old Testament and often involves vengeance or justice where it is translated "avenger of blood." This is no storybook prince role. This is someone deputized with a responsibility of upholding justice. The community would rely on a man like Boaz.

In many ancient Near Eastern societies, responsibility fell on the go'el to restore balance, a balance that was both moral and physical. Before Ruth came to Bethlehem, the Israelites had only recently come out of a season of severe imbalance, famine, and judgment. This belief in the scales of justice being tied to the land would be weighing heavily on the minds of those who experienced the previous lack.

But before we go further, there may be some, especially when reading the Old Testament, who question why God set up such a male-dominated society. Why can't Ruth simply take over Elimelech's land? Why did God require a man to be in charge? However, if we look closely at Scripture, we might be surprised to find that He didn't.

Genesis 3:16 tells us that inequality and distance between men and women is a result of the fall, and God mournfully tells Eve that now Adam will be the "dominant partner." Whereas before they were companions, meant to complement one another, now there will exist a hierarchy.

This, however, isn't God's design and in fact, throughout the Bible, He goes out of his way to use women in his grand narrative, in spite of the way society viewed them.

Ruth is a dramatic example of this, especially when we consider how unassuming she is in her actions. Though young and beautiful, Ruth is certainly not "on the prowl" but instead working a grueling and unglamorous job in the hot, desert sun. And since the story does not take place in a Hollywood set, I'm betting this was not Ruth's best look!

Her humility and willingness to serve God affords our narrator another opportunity to showcase God's plan for reconciliation, as Boaz lavished her with hospitality and protection. Only after Ruth returns to Naomi at the end of the day was he significantly connected to Ruth.

That evening, Ruth beat out the barley she had gleaned and carries home about eight pounds. When she shows Naomi, her shock is visible. In disbelief, Naomi asks where she gleaned that day. Ruth reminds her of their earlier conversation, of where she might be safest in Bethlehem, and says she had stayed in the part of the field belonging to Boaz the entire day.

Naomi smiles, saying, "That man is one of our closest relatives, one of our family redeemers" (Ruth 2:20).

"She worked hard throughout the seven weeks of the wheat and barley seasons until the harvest was complete in early summer" (Ruth 2:23).

The providence of gleaning in Boaz's field was no coincidence. In His Sermon on the Mount, Jesus tells us, "The humble will inherit the earth." I wonder if He thought about his once homeless ancestor, Ruth, as He was teaching. It was no coincidence that Ruth "happened" to glean in Boaz's field; she was precisely located there in God's plan for her life.

Naomi knew that harvest time involved late nights spent

winnowing. The threshing floor is where grain is taken for the purpose of winnowing, which basically means sorting out the good from the bad, the useable parts of the harvest from what will be discarded. But there is far greater significance to the threshing floor in the Old Testament. It's a storied past of sexual deviancy and Israelite failure.

Ruth has never seen this side of Naomi: fussing over her appearance, braiding her hair into extravagant coifs, and anointing her with perfume. Ruth feels a little like a doll. Naomi is even smiling for the first time in a long time, but her plan is making Ruth nervous. Proposing to Boaz? And on the threshing floor no less!

Mahlon had told Ruth the history behind the threshing room floor, which is where King Ahab and King Jehoshaphat once received the prophets' disastrous counsel, and where Hosea announced Israel's judgment. She could hear Mahlon's voice as he quoted the prophet: "You've prostituted yourself . . . You won't remain in the Eternal's land, and you can count on this: Ephraim will go back to slavery in Egypt" (Hos. 9:1, 3).

Her late husband would then tell her how the king became enraged and locked up the prophet of God to meet his doom—the consequence of not listening to the Almighty. The story was burned into Ruth's brain.

The plan was risky, to be sure. Was she about to become another tragic moment in history on the stage of the threshing floor? But Naomi insisted; the question remained, how much did Ruth trust Naomi?

In the beginning of Ruth 3, Naomi lays out her plan for Ruth and has apparently decided to play matchmaker. As we see in chapter two, Boaz is a kinsman redeemer, and Naomi instructs Ruth to propose marriage to Boaz. The plan is to present Ruth perfumed and looking her best to a sleepy, possibly inebriated, Boaz on the threshing room floor. Romantic, right?

Ruth feels a bit foolish lingering in the shadows while she watches Boaz eat and drink. It is well past dark before he finally does to lie down. Exhausted, he immediately falls into deep sleep—so much so that Ruth is easily able to uncover his feet and lie down there.

Naomi had explained that this was a symbolic gesture that Boaz would understand, and though it seems strange to Ruth, she trusts Naomi not to lead her astray. At midnight, a dream startles Boaz awake, but as he tries to regain his wits, he realizes it is no dream—at his feet is a young woman!

"Who are you?" Boaz deliriously inquires.

"It's me, Ruth." Then, remembering the phrase Naomi had made her practice, she says, "Spread your cloak over your servant, for you are my kinsman redeemer."

Boaz sits upright to look her in the eyes. He can't help but think how many other men Ruth could have captivated by her beauty. Certainly he had paid especial attention to her earlier in accordance with law but also because he had been immediately attracted to her. And now here she is, alone, and offering to marry him.

"Your loyalty is incredible. Everyone has been speaking of your character." For once, Boaz seems to be the one caught off-guard. He gazes intently at her before saying thoughtfully, "I will happily do all you say, but there is one other kinsman closer than I am. I must resolve this first."

Then, pleading with her to stay until morning, Boaz promises to get Ruth home so that no one would see her and spread rumors. Before she leaves the next morning, he proceeds to give her grain to take home to Naomi. He refuses to let her leave empty-handed.

Although it's easy to read impropriety into the way in which Ruth proposes to Boaz—in the evening after he had been drinking and it was dark—note his reaction. When Boaz first inquired about Ruth back in chapter two, he asked "whose" she was. In essence, who does she belong to? However, when she approaches him—boldly and all alone that night—he asks, "Who are you?"

Ruth's answer was characteristically humble, but there had clearly been a relationship forming, for Boaz's immediate response was to say, "You are a woman of noble character." Had Ruth been attempting to seduce Boaz, she was either entirely inept, which is unlikely for many reasons, or that was not her motive. Boaz made it clear that the latter is more accurate, for his response was to praise her character and then protect her from public scrutiny by having her leave before daylight.

In modern times it can be easy to miss the risk involved on Ruth's behalf. If someone were to have seen her that night, well, we can all imagine the tabloids. And with everyone fully aware of her Moabite heritage, she would no doubt be painted accordingly.

But Ruth once again courageously stepped out into God's providential plan as if she knew she could not fail! She had known loss, to be sure, but she nonetheless trusted in a plan much greater than her individual existence.

"For he is the son of your daughter-in-law who loves you and has been better to you than seven sons!" (Ruth 4:15)

Boaz took very seriously his responsibility to uphold justice as a go'el, and there was the law to consider. This required going to Elimelech's nearest kinsman. But because he very much wanted to marry Ruth, Boaz devised a plan.

As he waited by the city gate to ensure a crowd of witnesses, he was rehearsing in his mind how to present the situation to the kinsman nearer Naomi's late husband, Elimelech. He decided on a good news/bad news delivery, like "You inherited land . . . but there's a catch."

Boaz knew the kinsman would be interested in the land, but as he informed him of Ruth, he carefully phrased her as "the dead man's widow . . . the Moabite" (Ruth 4:5) and reminded the kinsman that this would retain Elimelech's name. At this, the kinsman gladly relinquished his right.

His plan worked: Boaz could now legally marry Ruth.

The book concludes with a son being born to Ruth and Boaz. The townspeople once again chimed in with chorus-like enthusiasm; however, they not only spoke of the child, but of the blessing Ruth had been to Naomi. They go so far as to declare Ruth "better than seven sons," a not insignificant number. Ruth wasn't just an example of faith in action for women but for all who believe.

Some scholars discredit Ruth as part of a divine plan, suggesting that she cared more about providing a son and perpetuating the patriarchy. In other words, her interest was not in following the one true God, but rather keeping women suppressed in male-dominated society.

Such shortsighted statements suggest that Ruth had no unity of purpose with the male figures in the lineage of David. Because God didn't overthrow a sexist society in order to achieve His purpose does not mean He wasn't at work through Ruth's obedience. And God's providential hand should not be confused with ignorance or an absence of faith on Ruth's part, because it is a sign of true covenantal faith. When society got it wrong, God got it right, and Ruth had the faith to trust Him.

God's plan may not unfold the easy way or the way we would like, but our responsibility as believers is to follow Him regardless, which is exactly what Ruth did. God isn't interested in establishing an earthly kingdom where the priority is noble blood. God establishes His kingdom through faith.

"And they named him Obed. He became the father of Jesse and the grandfather of David" (Ruth 4:17).

Boaz and Ruth stand back and marvel. Naomi is transfixed. Tenderly pressing her wrinkled face into his pudgy cheeks, she is enraptured. For Naomi, no other humans exist. This boy is all that mattered.

Holding their baby is giving her new life, which Ruth had watched taken from Naomi back in Moab, and is now being restored. She and Ruth had faced considerable adversity, but watching her now was like watching her reborn. She dances around their home, child in arms, happily performing any household chores, never failing to remember the woman whose faith has carried her when she could not imagine the way on her own.

Some scholars question Ruth's theological role in the overall book because she makes no explicit prayers. They relegate her to the realm of biological necessity, merely a womb to carry an heir, suggesting that although she is the main character, she is only coincidentally aligned with God's will and doesn't consciously follow Yahweh.

However, Ruth plainly declared her allegiance: "Your God will be my God" (Ruth 1:16). This is hardly an unconscious decision. Ruth then followed through with her actions. James 2:26 says, "Just as the body is dead without breath, so also faith is dead without good works." Ruth's faith was clearly alive!

It seems the entire town has come to celebrate this new life! Those who had once regarded Ruth as a stranger and possible threat to their community are now singing her praises. Food and gifts are piled on every surface, and all gather to admire this tiny baby boy.

In their admiration, they name Ruth's son Obed, meaning

"worship." What no one realizes on that day was that this baby boy would be the grandfather of King David.

Note that Ruth or Boaz didn't name Obed; the community did. Here the community recognized the significance of one child's birth. The final scene of Ruth is a beautiful picture of those people of faith (represented by Ruth) being united with their redeemer (represented by Boaz), thereby made full through the gift of new life.

The author of Ruth made a brilliant parallel to the ultimate Redeemer, Jesus, and His bride, the church, who through faith are given new life. The author's structuring of the narrative was intentional, a technical flourish that expresses a theological concept.

When hard times hit, and Jesus assures us they will, our response should be one that turns our attention to God. In John 16:33 Jesus says, "In this world you will be plagued with times of trouble . . . but you need not fear; I have triumphed over this corrupt world order." In this way, the book of Ruth reminds us that faith keeps us in the providential hand of God.

Faith connects us to the unchanging One in the midst of turmoil. Some will argue that because of the chauvinistic and patriarchal society of ancient times, women performed relatively unimportant roles in the Bible. Although their status was unquestionably low in ancient society, God made a point of using women in very critical, monumental ways. In fact, both Ruth and Rahab establish a promised redemption—not only for Israel as a nation, but the whole world. They are key figures for understanding the New Covenant.

The enemy wants us to believe the same lie of invisibility, that we can only perform relatively unimportant roles in ministry. Often people are overlooked based solely on their race; being different can mean being excluded, and women rarely are treated fairly or equally to their male counterparts in ministry. However, such actions are not biblical. Society doesn't get to say what God's plan is.

What is biblical is following God even when a significant amount of self-sacrifice is required, when believing something that looks and feels impossible is called for, when faith like Ruth's is necessary.

Reflection

1. Do you ever find yourself trying to bargain with God? Do you offer to obey, but only if He changes something in your life first?

2. What are some situations in your life that seem unfair?

3. We glimpse an even fuller picture of the magnitude of Ruth's legacy when the author makes a striking connection to Jesus. In the previous chapter, when Ruth returns to tell Naomi about her encounter with Boaz, there is a direct parallel to the woman at the well. Ruth 3:16 says, "Ruth told Naomi everything Boaz had done for her." Compare this to the testimony of the woman at the well: "Come and see a man who told me everything I ever did!" (John 4:29)

4. Consider how this literary technique of drawing parallels is frequently used in Scripture and gives us a better understanding of what faith like Ruth's can accomplish. Because of her faithfulness, an heir was born for Israel that would unite all nations.

5. What is the most uncomfortable thing you've ever done in faith?

6. Do you find it hard to obey without knowing the "plan"?

7. Do you see yourself as a victim or as actively surrendering yourself to God's will?

8. Though the practice of a kinsman redeemer was rather familiar in ancient Near Eastern legal systems, consider how the Bible uses it to illustrate how Jesus redeems mankind.

9. What are some situations in your life that have made you feel bitter as Naomi did at the beginning of Ruth?

10. Do you find it hard to believe that your life is part of a divine story? If yes, why?

RAHAB WALKS THE TALK

Chapter 5: An Unexpected Ally

"Salmon, the father of Boaz by Rahab" (Matt. 1:5 ESV).

"There has not arisen a prophet since in Israel like Moses, whom the Lord knew face to face" (Deut. 34:10 ESV).

"Be strong and courageous" (Josh. 1:6–7, 9).

History of frustration (Num. 14:6)

Chapter 6: A Woman with a Plan

"And in the same way, was not also Rahab the prostitute justified by works when she received the messengers and sent them out another way?" (James 2:25 ESV)

Joshua 2:9–11; Exodus 15:15

Hebrews 11:31

Chapter 5

An Unexpected Ally

When reading the Scriptures, we find some unexpected characters listed in the genealogy of Christ. Ancient genealogies rarely included any mention of women. Paternity was what counted, and that was how the "royal bloodline" was maintained.

In the book of Matthew, the author presents a rather more inclusive genealogical account. His deviation is important to consider, and in the first chapter we find not one but four women listed, all of whom are of questionable backgrounds. Tamar, from Genesis 38, sold herself, disguised as a prostitute, to her father-in-law. Ruth was from the forbidden tribe of Moabites, Bathsheba was the object of King David's murderous affair, recorded in both 2 Samuel and 1 Kings. And Rahab was a Canaanite prostitute.

So, what's the point? Why would Matthew want to sully the lineage of the Messiah with so many unscrupulous characters? The answer, just like life, is not that simple. Each one of these women are part of a larger plan.

Where society would have labeled them rejects, God saw purpose and potential. Society kept them on the outskirts, but God brought them into His family—the very lineage of His only begotten Son. Each of them were brought into the fold—not by genetics but by faith. Once again, this is a story within a story, the individuals ultimately part of a larger picture.

*"I will be with you just as I was with Moses, and I will never
fail or abandon you"* (Josh. 1:5).

Joshua was now the leader of the entire nation of Israel, and
he had never felt more alone. Moses had anointed him, and he
had no doubt God's presence was with him, but he also knew he
was no Moses.

Moses had walked with God in the literal sense, not simply
metaphorical. Who could compare? And more than that, Joshua
knew the stiff-necked people he was leading. Although they were
his people, God's chosen people, they had proven even under
Moses' leadership how easily they strayed. Even Moses' nephews
had gone against the Lord, going so far as to violate the holiest
place in the temple. If the sons of the high priest can't be relied
on, who can?

Joshua wanted to be brave. To witness miracles. But leading
Israel was a double-edged sword. He knew that on one side God
assured victory, while on the other, mankind was prone to wander.
He knew the patience Moses had exhibited. He saw the constant
mediation. More than once, he had watched even Moses lose his
temper.

Now the responsibility lay squarely on Joshua's broad
shoulders. In many ways, Joshua preferred being a soldier and following orders, but now was not the time for hesitation. In the
desert plains, beneath the veil of midnight, Joshua knew that the
time had come to take the land that should have been theirs forty
years prior.

Our story picks up after the death of Moses, the greatest prophet Israel will ever know. Deuteronomy 34:10 says, "There has
not arisen a prophet since in Israel like Moses, whom the Lord
knew face to face." Joshua has been watching closely.
Commissioned by God, he was present with Moses in the Tent

of Meeting as the pillar of God's very presence hovered outside.

Joshua had walked the rugged, steep-walled peaks of Mount Sinai with Moses when God met with him; he has seen incredible things! Scripture clearly shows that Joshua has big faith. When Moses sends twelve spies into Canaan, their Promised Land, Joshua is one of only two who believed that taking the land is possible. The other ten pathetically replied, "The land is highly desirable, but the people who already live there are really strong" (Num. 14:27–28).

Although the Canaanites likely appeared intimidating—the Israelites described them as giants—but Joshua was so outraged by their cowardice that he tore his clothes and began to argue with them. The argument got so heated that the Israelites threatened to stone him! They refused to listen. Joshua had wasted his breath. Clearly the Israelites would rather go back to slavery in Egypt than to trust God and conquer the land He had promised them.

Rather than argue with the stiff-necked Israelites, Moses talked to God. Instead of obliterating them, God told Moses that the Israelites would wander, homeless, for forty years. No one over the age of twenty would live to enter the Promised Land, and no one of the generation unwilling to have faith and obey would be allowed to enjoy this land "flowing with milk and honey."

But God made an exception for Joshua and Caleb, the two spies with faith who were obedient to God. And it is Joshua who was ultimately chosen to lead the people into the land of Canaan and to conquer the city of Jericho, a city that would have stood out as a remarkably imposing structure in the ancient world.

Would this time be any different?

The plan is to enter Jericho through an inn situated on the very exterior of the city that is run by a local prostitute. If they could slip into the seedy environment, they should be able to go undetected on their reconnaissance mission.

Instead of twelve, Joshua chooses only two spies to penetrate the mighty brick wall surrounding Jericho. As he is assessing his choices, Joshua feels skeptical. The two men are currently standing outside their tents joking, as if it is an ordinary day. No preparation is taking place, and no praying.

Their wives have packed some provisions for their journey, and Joshua watches as they sloppily eat their food before beginning their trek. Self-awareness clearly is sorely lacking. In addition, Joshua has already had to repeat his instructions—never a good sign—and, although they are physically prepared, Joshua is concerned they are more brawn than brain.

Hoping he has overlooked some other more worthy candidate, Joshua examines his troops one last time, only to reluctantly confirm that of all his men, these are the best suited for the task.

"Jehovah Jireh . . ." Joshua prays silently as he sends them off to Jericho.

The danger of spying is not only getting caught but also jeopardizing an entire mission. Joshua would have certainly been concerned for the lives of his men, but as a commander, he would have had to consider the success of the mission. Having been a spy himself, Joshua would have known the task before them and certainly understood the hazards.

Joshua would have also undoubtedly been reiterating the past, reminding Israel of the consequences of not having faith in God's plan. God told him to "be strong and courageous" three times in Joshua 1.

This phrase is echoed throughout the Bible. In the New Testament, Paul urged the believers in Corinth: "Be courageous. Be strong" (1 Cor. 16:13). As Christians, even when walking squarely in the middle of God's plan, we only see or understand in part. We need reminding that the battle in front of us will require courage and often will require all of our strength.

Joshua would have been well aware of the two he was sending into battle. He would have witnessed many times how unreliable the Israelites could be; yet, he also knew that God was not dependent on man to accomplish His purposes. What he didn't know was that God had an unexpected ally waiting on the other side of the wall.

Within the fortified walls of the city, freshwater springs fed elaborate gardens. Flowering vines crept across arbors and added to the allure of a city center filled with Egyptian artwork, accumulated over centuries of trade between the mighty empires.

Riches of every kind filled the mighty walls that had never been breached, for though an oasis in the desert, Jericho was not complacent in their wealth. They were well aware of the Israelites and vigilante in surveillance. Israel was barely a nation, but they had defeated some powerful enemies, which was making the Canaanites uneasy.

Lately there had been quite a stir at the inn. Everyone was talking about the Jordan River, how the God of the Israelites supposedly stopped the flow of the river so they could walk across. Some were comparing it to the parting of the Red Sea decades earlier.

Rahab listened well. In her profession, talking was not appreciated. As a prostitute, people came to her for lodging and sexual favors, not advice or conversation. But she listened eagerly whenever the subject of Yahweh came up. Mentally taking notes, Rahab had committed to memory certain phrases she noticed being repeated.

They may not have had social media, and the passage of information may have taken considerably more time than it does today, but word did spread. For a nation as powerful and connected as Canaan, word of the Israelites was news that would have merited particular attention.

In fact, the Canaanites would have undoubtedly been paying attention to Israel, considering the massive amount of trade they did with Egypt. After all, the enemy of my friend is my enemy, right?

Besides, the Canaanites would have known that they were at odds with the Israelites' belief system. The Canaanites were polytheistic, believing in multiple gods, and many of their practices were abhorrent to the Israelites and a consistent source of trepidation. Apostasy, which is refusing to continue to follow a religious faith, is a recurrent theme in the Old Testament. The Israelite's first recorded abandonment of faith is immediately following their deliverance from slavery in Egypt. Anyone recall the golden calf?

When staying true to Yahweh, the Israelites looked quite different from other nations. One God, no idols—a stark contrast to other Near Eastern nations. However, often the temptation to be like other nations proved too much, and throughout the Old Testament, we witness a struggle to be "in the world and not of it." To not fit in.

This struggle is one that we face to this day, although it looks slightly different. In 1 John 2:15, Christians are urged not to "love the world or the things in the world." When we are more concerned with fitting in or being received by the world, we compromise our walk with Christ. Just as He is calling us today, God was calling the Israelites to Himself, setting them apart. What the Israelites had not yet understood was that their chosen status wasn't about race. God was building a kingdom of faith.

Rahab had lived in Jericho her whole life, but it was not much of a life. In the land of Canaan, if you weren't a shrine prostitute, you were disposable. In fact, her home was in the city wall, the farthest place from the town center as possible. If your services weren't being called on, you weren't supposed to be seen. And Rahab had become an expert at making herself invisible.

Living in the city wall wasn't so bad, though. In fact, the massive edifice was her favorite space. The walls were so thick that she used her window ledge as a bench seat. There Rahab would sit and think about the rumors. She picked up phrases from passing strangers. "All the inhabitants of Canaan have melted away."

Suddenly, as she looked out over the desert, she saw two men suspiciously approaching Jericho.

Rahab's character has been about as impugned as imaginable. The Midrash, the ancient rabbinic interpretation of Scripture, is replete with salacious interpretations of her story. Her very name was often twisted into an innuendo-based slur. In fact, this preoccupation with our main character's occupation easily obscures her purpose.

The authors of Scripture make clear that she was a prostitute. This detail is repeatedly provided. Rahab was a three-time outsider: a woman, a Canaanite, and a prostitute. The only way she could have been a less appealing hero is if she were afflicted with leprosy!

What is also made clear is that her role in the overall narrative of Scripture is essential for our understanding as believers. Rahab was about to showcase a level of wisdom and faith that proves transformational for this chosen Israelite army.

Reflection

1. Have you ever felt like a social reject and doubted whether God could use you?

2. Are you intentional about including others? Why or why not?

3. Do you expect to be disappointed by others? Why? How does this influence your leadership?

4. Do you compare yourself to other leaders?

5. Rahab is one of many women depicted as "looking through a window." However, while Rahab is of the lowest social rank, most all other examples in Scripture are of royal and highly revered women. In fact, in Proverbs 7:6, even Lady Wisdom is depicted as looking through a window.

6. Have you ever ruled yourself out of an opportunity based on your qualifications?

7. Imagine for a moment you're Joshua. You were willing to go to war forty years prior, but because of the lack of faith of those around you, you've been forced to live in the wilderness for forty years. How would you handle the responsibility of leading the charge on Jericho?

8. Imagine for a moment you're Rahab. You know the two men coming toward Jericho are rather incompetent spies and will likely see your place as a good place to blend in. Do you seize the opportunity or play it safe and turn them in to the king, who will undoubtedly be on their trail?

Chapter 6

A Woman with a Plan

Harvesting time has arrived, and Rahab knows exactly where to hide the incompetent spies. Taking them to the rooftop, Rahab pulls back stalks of flax. "Here, get under!" Once she is sure they are properly hidden, Rahab brushes any dried flax off her yellow dress and hurries downstairs.

She knows the king's soldiers will appear any moment, so she resumes her usual duties so as not to raise any suspicion. Scarcely any time has passed when a fist pounds on her door.

Rahab smooths her long, uncovered black hair and casually opens the door, as though she has not sensed the urgency of the knock.

"Bring out the spies! We know they came here!"

Looming over Rahab, the king's soldiers are an imposing pair. Physically incomparable, the king has his pick of the men of Jericho, and he chooses well. Clearly, they are confident in their mission, and both are armed accordingly. Their accusatory tone tells Rahab that they plan to ambush her with their knowledge, logically leading to her surrendering the spies.

Rahab, however, is not surprised they had this intel, so she does not betray any confidence as she calmly assures them that, yes, that is indeed true. The two Israeli men have come to her inn. She then says, "I didn't know where they were from, though. When it was getting dark, before the gate was closed, they left. If you hurry, you will surely overtake them!"

The king's soldiers glance at one another, then nod at Rahab and leave. As they hurry off in vain pursuit of the spies, Rahab returns to the roof.

Many scholars have struggled with Rahab's lie in this scene, but when taken in consideration of her life and cultural background, it's hardly surprising that she was able to deceive so easily. This was a woman who had no previous contact with the Word of God or the things of God, except what she gathered from passing strangers. We can hardly expect someone who had no knowledge of the ways of God to behave according to them.

Furthermore, the lie itself was not praised in Scripture, just recorded. It was a quick-witted woman's response in defense of God's people.

Trembling, Rahab lifts the stalks of flax and whispers into the night air, "I know the Lord has given this land to you."

The spies glance at one another. They have been lying on the roof in silence since she left them, too afraid to move or say anything. They assume she will turn them in to the king. The last thing they expect from a prostitute is a profession of faith.

"All who live in this country are melting in fear because of you," she continues, reciting phrases she has heard that she knows are connected to Yahweh. "Your God is God in heaven and on earth below!"

The spies stammer for words, but Rahab continues, "Please! Promise me that you will show kindness to me and my family, as I have shown you. Spare our lives. Save us from death!" she pleads.

The men nod. "Our lives for your lives. Don't breathe a word of what we're doing, and we will treat you kindly when God gives us this land."

Rahab nods and assures them that she will tell no one, then

urges them to leave by way of the hills, for she knows which route the king's men will take. She gives them some suggestions on how to be more inconspicuous this time and says, "Hide for three days, until the king's men return, and then go on your way!"

The men make her promise to tie a red cord on her window—a way of designating her home as allied territory—and tell her to make sure all members of her family are in her home when their army comes. That way they can assure their survival. The spies make clear that anyone who is not in her home, which is marked by a scarlet thread, will die.

The Bible doesn't flatter these two men or promote their spying prowess. In fact, the two men are discovered the very day they arrive and are rescued by a prostitute. They spend their entire mission hiding and following her directions. Their mission was to scout out the land, which clearly does not happen. What could they possibly tell Joshua?

After three days hiding in the honeycombed caves that Rahab had advised them of on the outskirts of Jericho, the men return to camp. They go straight to Joshua, but as soon as others see they had returned, it feels as though the entire camp has gathered. All are anxiously awaiting details about Jericho—details the two men do not have.

They proceed to explain how the soldiers had immediately spotted them and how they assumed they were going to die. Then they relay Rahab's words verbatim: "I know that the Lord has given this land to you and that a great fear of you has fallen on us . . . We have heard how the Lord dried up the water of the Red Sea for you when you came out of Egypt, and what you did to Sihon and Og, the two kings of the Amorites east of the Jordan, whom you completely destroyed. When we heard of it, our hearts melted and everyone's courage failed because of you, for the Lord your God is God in heaven above and on earth below."

Joshua listens to their words, stunned. Did they hear themselves? Rahab had recited the very words God had spoken to Moses! The Israelites continue to press the spies for information on Jericho, but Joshua doesn't bother lingering. He's heard all he needs to—he's heard from God.

This was better than insider information. This was confirmation and Joshua knows it. Rahab weaves particular phrases into her speech that come from Exodus and Deuteronomy. In Exodus 23:27 God tells the Israelites that He will send his "terror" ahead of them. In Exodus 15:15 He says that the inhabitants of Canaan have "melted away" in fear, and the phrase Rahab stated regarding God being "God in heaven and on the earth below," was straight from Deuteronomy 4:39.

Her speech told Joshua they had a man on the inside—or rather, a woman on the inside. Furthermore, her profession of faith was backed with action. The Bible makes clear that true faith will be accompanied by deeds. James 2:17 tells us that faith without works is dead. Using Abraham as his example, James goes on to say, "Faith was completed by his works." In the same way, each one of Rahab's pronouncements of faith was backed by works. Even the scarlet thread was hung in her window, but not even Joshua knew how significant this symbol would be.

An excited buzz spreads at camp, and anticipation is building. The Israelites have been eating nothing but manna on their journey through the wilderness, but the day after Passover, as they camp in the plains of Jericho, Joshua has them taste the produce of the land. To build their enthusiasm, Joshua wants them to sense how close they are.

He, however, is thoughtful. Earnestly he seeks answers from

God on how to proceed each day. One day, while he is walking alone near Jericho, he looks up to see a man standing in front of him, a sword drawn in his hand.

"Are you for us or for our enemies?" Joshua asks, instinctively preparing to draw his weapon but knowing there would not be enough time.

"Neither" he replies, much to Joshua's confusion. "But as commander of the Lord's army, I have now come."

Immediately, Joshua falls on his face in reverence to the heavenly being. "What message does my Lord have for his servant?"

"Take off your sandals, for the place you are standing is holy."

Joshua had gone to great lengths to ensure his people were following covenantal law. He went so far in chapter five as to circumcise any men who were not circumcised in the wilderness. Joshua was a great leader, but as we read, it's easy to see the pressure of following Moses.

This makes the moment the angel appeared all the more meaningful, as Joshua would have been desperately seeking answers. They were about to face down the Canaanites on their home turf, but how? The words the angel speaks are the same words God once told Moses when He met him at the burning bush—something that Joshua would have surely not missed.

Rahab did not have the benefit of a wise leader or an angelic encounter. She had a red ribbon hanging on her window and the word of two amateur spies. But God was about to test the faith of His people. Immediately following the scene with the angel of God's army, God gave Joshua the battle plan. His instructions, however, were a bit unconventional.

"So . . . we walk around the city and then start playing music?" The skeptical stares are combined only with uncomfortable silence. Joshua is doing his best to convey what God had told him, but the plan is basically just that—to walk around the city carrying trumpets for an entire week. Thereafter, the Israelites will blow their horns and shout loudly. This is a new one.

"There's a specific order to it," Joshua says, but who was he kidding? He can't make this sound intimidating or logical. This plan was all about Israel trusting God. Interrupting the anxious whispers, Joshua says, "Don't you remember the words of our great prophet, Moses?"

The tribe becomes silent at the mention of Moses.

"We were scared as we stood before the Red Sea! Pharoah's army was coming for us! We thought slavery or death were our only options. But Moses told us, 'The Lord will fight for you; you need only to be still.' Those words didn't make sense! Be still? How do you defeat an army being still? Then we watched as God parted an entire sea and used those same walls of water to crush our enemy! The same wall that held back the waters claimed our victory!"

The Israelites stare as Joshua's voice cracks with emotion. His body shakes as he says, "We have to have faith! God has given us this land!"

A single man steps forward toward Joshua, and placing a fist on his chest, solemnly takes a knee, demonstrating his allegiance. Another follows, and another, until the entire nation of Israel pledges to follow Joshua into battle, no matter what their plan looked or sounded like.

Can you imagine? Joshua and every person gathered had grown up hearing the stories. They may have been old enough to remember the first time they had been given the Promised Land but were too scared to enter. It looked impossible then too.

This time, taking Jericho looked impossible, and the plan

sounded utterly ridiculous. Although we don't know exactly how Joshua rallied the troops, I can only imagine him showing them the parallel that this isn't all that different from before. The victory is all God's; what He asks of us is faith.

So far, the army are marching. Around and around and around. For days they have done nothing but march. Jericho is on lockdown, no one is allowed in, and no one is allowed out. And the king's army has no idea what the marching means. Do they attack first? What is Israel's move here exactly? No one seems to know.

Rahab watches as her family becomes increasingly doubtful. The incessant circling looks like child's play. Confused, Rahab's brother shouts, "What on earth is their plan?"

But Rahab has no answer. She certainly had not expected this, but stories of parted seas fill her mind and stir her faith. After the spies left, Rahab stockpiled provisions just in case the battle went on for many days. She remembers what they had said about anyone who left her house not being protected: "Their blood would be on their own heads." Anxiously, she tries to calm her brother and feels somehow responsible for him, though she knows the choice to believe is his alone.

Blood is an important motif in Scripture. An incredible weight is associated with it, to the point where God says that it pollutes the land, and He won't dwell on defiled land. In Numbers, God tells Moses plainly, "Bloodshed pollutes the land . . . Do not defile the land where you live and where I dwell, for I, the Lord, dwell among the Israelites."

Now, it might seem contradictory to tell the Israelites not to kill and then send them into battle, but if we watch carefully, God had been working behind the scenes to redeem a nation that stood opposed to Him. He had even turned a prostitute's heart toward Him. So, when the Israelite spies told Rahab that those who don't show their faith by staying in the protected space take their lives in their own hands, we see provision being made—an offer to turn from evil to God.

The people of Canaan had a choice—trust God or trust the defenses of man. Rahab made her choice for herself and her family.

More than once Rahab had insisted on her family not leaving, but they did not share her certainty. The morning of the seventh day, the Israelites begin their march. Rahab's brother stands up, saying abruptly, "This is ridiculous! What is their plan—to make us dizzy?" Rahab has no answer.

"I'm leaving," he says, walking for the door.

"No!" Rahab shrieks, lunging in front of him.

"You can't be serious," he says, annoyed, shoving her away.

Just then, the army blows their trumpets. The sound is deafening. Time feels suspended and the hairs on the back of Rahab's neck stand on end. Everyone races towards the window as the Israelites raise a loud shout and the earth begins to tremble. Dishes fall off the table, furniture topples over, and everyone is thrown to the ground. The walls begin to crack, and as Rahab looks up, she watches the mighty wall of Jericho implode. Brick by brick, it crumbles down to the foundations. Her home is the only evidence it ever existed.

God had given Jericho over to his people, and Rahab and her family are among the redeemed.

"To the faithful you show yourself faithful; to those with integrity you show integrity" (Ps. 18:25).

At the center of this narrative, we find faith, the connection between God and His people—their response to Him. The Israelites were still God's people while they were wandering in the wilderness, but God had so much better for them than a life of homelessness.

The Israelites clearly struggled to let go of what would have seemed normal and were constantly wanting to be like the other nations around them. But God pushes them to relinquish that and let Him take control of their lives. Doing so required an act of faith.

Rahab was all about action. Her story began as an "other." She wasn't a major player in Canaanite society, but she was certainly no Israelite. She wouldn't have had any natural reason to believe she ever would be, which is what made her faith so incredibly remarkable. This faith is what God rewards.

In Psalms 18:25, David wrote that God shows Himself faithful to those who are faithful. In other words, God isn't a tyrant. When we serve Him and go to battle for Him, He repays our loyalty. The Israelites are rewarded with a home and freedom, and Rahab likewise joins a new family, a new kingdom.

She had no promise of being included with God's chosen people, yet she proclaimed the truth. Doing so lands herself squarely in the heart of God's redemptive plan. We watch as she guided Israel's spies to safety and boldly misdirects the Canaanite soldiers.

Those same soldiers would have undoubtedly protected her if she had turned in the spies, and if they had discovered her ruse, she would have certainly been killed as a collaborator. She risked everything. Her faith was her defining trait, visible in every action recorded in Joshua.

Ironically, the heroine of the story is underestimated by everyone except God. She could not have imagined that her act of faith would land her in the biblical "hall of fame." In the New Testament, James mentioned her in the same breath as Abraham, and Paul put her faith on par with the army of Israel. That's like comparing a mathematician to Einstein or a local basketball player with Michael Jordan.

Israel was at its very beginning when Rahab stepped into the picture. Forty years was a long time to wander in the desert, but it was not a long time in terms of forming a nation. Tragic failures and monumental victories are throughout the Old Testament, but ultimately, none of these stories is about the individual characters. They're about a God who sees each and every heart and makes a way for His flawed creation to belong.

Reflection

1. In the ancient Near East a common way of making a judicial "guilty or innocent verdict" was a trial by water. If the person thrown into the water was able to avoid drowning, they were innocent. The belief in this method stemmed from their allegiance to Baal, who conquered the sea god. Consider how God used both the Red Sea and the Jordan River as a way of proving His authority to those who were following false gods.

2. Do your expectations of others match their understanding of God?

3. Consider how Rahab's faith might have influenced her son, Boaz.

4. Like the scarlet cord Rahab hung in her window, what are some symbols in your life of times God has come through for you?

5. Do you struggle to follow an unconventional plan?

6. What is your metaphorical Jericho? What is holding you back from total obedience?

7. What do your actions say about your faith?

8. Do you care more about fitting in or following God?

DEBORAH TOLD YA SO

Chapter 7: As Bleak as It Sounds

"Deborah, the wife of Lappidoth, was a prophet who was judging Israel at the time" (Judg. 4:4).

"The Lord will sell Sisera into the hand of a woman" (Judg. 4:9 ESV).

Judges 4:10–17

"Deborah said to Barak, 'Up! For this is the day in which the Lord has given Sisera into your hand. Does not the Lord go out before you?' So Barak went down from Mount Tabor with ten thousand men following him" (Judg. 4:14 ESV).

Chapter 8: No R.E.S.P.E.C.T.

Judges 4:10–24; 5:1–31

"As Barak was pursuing Sisera, Jael went out to meet him and said to him, 'Come and I will show you the man whom you are seeking'" (Judg. 4:22 ESV).

"The earth trembled and the heavens dropped" (Judg. 4:4 Voice).

"Arise, Barak! Lead your captives away, son of Abinoam!" (Judg. 5:12)

"'May all who love you rise like the sun in all its power!' Then there was peace in the land for forty years" (Judg. 5:31).

Longer than the years of subservience: Deborah served twenty years.

Chapter 7

As Bleak as It Sounds

The period of Judges chronicles generations of failure on behalf of the Israelites—a failure to stay faithful to God. Often, we pass over talk of "idol worship," picturing in our heads little stone figurines like the kind you would buy from a kitschy gift shop. But the idolatry of ancient Canaan involved far more than trinkets, ranging from temple prostitution to child sacrifice (babies murdered on altars). The people gave themselves over to demonic forces.

Many have studied the violence of the Old Testament and concluded that God is a God of war. May we differentiate the motives of man and the heart of God. The battle that God was using people like Deborah to wage was not against people, but against the forces that they were allowing to enslave them.

"Deborah, the wife of Lappidoth, was a prophet who was judging Israel at the time" (Judg. 4:4).

The title of "Judges" is pretty much a disclaimer. You know before ever reading a word that this is probably not the best season in the life of Israel. As I read Judges, I can't help but think of the words of Dickens—this was "the worst of times" for God's people. We enter the story after the death of Joshua, a great leader, who failed to train an heir.

In summary: Moses led the people through the wilderness to Canaan, the people rebelled and wandered aimlessly and homelessly for an entire generation. Then, just before Moses dies, God appoints Joshua. He proceeds to lead them into the Promised Land, and they conquered just as God said they would. There are many highs and lows as Israel struggles to follow God. Then Joshua dies and once again the people rebel.

Judges showcases the failures of mankind in pretty much every way, but most notably the people repeatedly fall into apostasy. Apostasy, as noted before, means "abandoning your faith." Now, it can vary greatly in severity, but in the period of history we're looking at, it's pretty extreme.

The false gods Israel kept turning to involved barbarous forms of worship, everything from church-sanctioned prostitution to human sacrifice. Yet, out of this grim period in history, God raises a select few to guide his people and deliver them from their enemies. One of these leaders is Deborah.

The people knew where to find her—she was always beneath the palm tree. She hadn't gone seeking the role of judge, but it was clear to the people that God spoke to her, and when people listened to her, their lives invariably improved.

At that time, the people of Israel were tent-dwellers, a pastoral community. They hadn't been organized enough since the day they conquered Canaan to truly establish a city. Constantly quarrelling and turning to false gods had taken their toll; it had cost Israel years of captivity. Then came Deborah.

The people of Israel had no central king, but the prophetess Deborah had proven her worth in speaking God's word and uniting the people. She did not meddle or try to involve herself in their troubles. Instead, the people saw her as someone they could go to, and that's precisely what they did.

Deborah was introduced as a prophetess and surely no greater responsibility could be given than to deliver God's word to His people. Though commonly interpreted as "wife of Lappidoth," this introductory line could also be interpreted as "woman of torches," suggesting the potency of her spiritual force and not referring to her husband. Whatever translation you align with, her husband and children are not the focus at any point. After this point, Lappidoth is never again mentioned in Scripture, and no children are ever recorded. The narrator clearly wants our attention on Deborah.

To say that it is unusual for a woman in the ancient world to hold a judicial seat would be an understatement. Yet, clearly, Deborah was a commanding force. In fact, she was the only judge in the entire Hebrew Bible who actually judged, and her counsel was so sought after that her presence on the battlefield was requested. In Judges 4:8 Barak was so insistent on her joining him that he refused to go without her!

Deborah lived at a time in Israel's history where it would have been easy to conform or be swayed and to deviate from the Torah, from God's provisional law for His people. After all, that is the overwhelming narrative of the book of Judges. Instead, she rose above, and God used her to not only lead His people in wisdom, but also rescue them from their enemies in battle.

"For the Lord will sell Sisera into the hand of a woman" (Judg. 4:9 ESV).

Though all come to her for wisdom, there are few Deborah herself can confide in; the people of Israel are her children, not her friends. She has been charged with guiding them in God's truth—teaching them how to follow His law, reprimanding them when necessary, and patiently helping them understand.

But leadership can be lonely, and seeing things others don't can be as much a curse as a blessing. She is anticipating Barak's response to their next course of action, and her heart is heavy. He's still afraid and Deborah knows he doesn't feel ready. Nonetheless, the time has come. Deborah is about to give her commander both the greatest hour of victory, while simultaneously withholding from him the credit, though undoubtedly if he had been able to see what she could, the victory over Sisera would have been the story of Barak.

As an adoptive mother with no biological children, I've been told I'm not a "real mother." I've been told that I won't know true purpose until I have given birth to children of my own. A comment of this nature has brought me to tears more than once, but I've come to realize that is not the biblical truth of motherhood at all.

Deborah was depicted as a mother. The *Voice* translation quotes her as saying, "I arose as a mother." But her children were the children of Israel. We have to then ask ourselves, "What is the true definition of motherhood?"

In modern society, mothers face a confusing dichotomy of opinions. A seemingly endless stream of unsolicited advice abounds, and no matter how progressive society becomes, the suggestion is still that you can't be a strong woman of leadership in any professional sphere and still be a good mother. Deborah defied this, taking on the roles of prophetess, judge, and military strategist.

One of the difficulties when studying Scripture as a woman is that the primary textual sources, the entire recognized canon of Scripture, was authored by men. And gender influences an author's perspective. As a woman, I am inherently more empathetic to women because I am a woman; therefore, I have experiences that inform my perspective. Keep this in mind when reading about motherhood in the Bible.

That said, Deborah's account was not coming from someone who would be interested in inflating the details or making her seem more heroic than she was. There is no conflict of interest. So, when we observe that the predominant qualities in this maternal figure are her strength, intelligence, and boldness of faith, it becomes clear that God's idea of a good mother is someone who leads with courage, who offers wisdom to those in need, and who protects those who trust her.

"Deborah said to Barak, 'Up! For this is the day in which the Lord has given Sisera into your hand. Does not the Lord go out before you?'" (Judg. 4:14 ESV)

Deborah was not easily agitated. Although she would be described by most as high spirited, she was also methodical. As passionate a leader as Deborah was, she was not impulsive. On this particular day, however, she called for her commander, Barak. The message was urgent, but her mighty warrior was clearly hesitating.

It's not as though Deborah wasn't aware that the Israelites were severely outmatched. She understood that while Sisera's army were armed with spears and riding on chariots, the Israelites were mostly on foot with handheld swords. But Deborah also knew that they would never be free as long as they cowered and lived in fear. God was calling them out, and Deborah refused to wait idly by.

I often find myself getting frustrated when helping my kids with their homework. Kids do not typically appreciate the fact that you work hard to send them to the best school, where they're assuredly challenged! Growth and obstacles can be frustrating.

Besides, a child doesn't often grasp the accomplishment on the other side of hard work. When I know my child isn't putting forth their best, it can be easy to just scold, rather than encourage. Sisera and the Canaanite's military superiority would have made victory over them seem impossible to the Israelites. For example, the Israelites were outnumbered nine hundred to zero in terms of chariots. In fact, the Bible recounts many times they had fought the Canaanites previously and failed. Yet Deborah showed no hesitation in rallying for battle.

Barak, however, was avoiding going into battle with the Canaanite army. He had insisted on Deborah's presence on the battlefield, even though she never actually engaged in combat. In Judges 4:14, his fear was once again visible, and it was as though Deborah was giving a rally cry or pumping Barak up for the finale. The ESV translation says, "Deborah said to Barak, 'Up! For this is the day in which the Lord has given Sisera into your hand.'"

She commanded him to get up so we can know that he was not then doing what was necessary. As his leader, she had reason to feel disappointed. We can all relate to feeling let down by someone. The question is, what is our response? In our agitation, do we do it ourselves or maybe internalize our frustration in order to avoid conflict?

Deborah's response was the alternative. Her feelings of disappointment were justified; however, she didn't merely scold him. She also made clear the opportunity before him was to be a part of something so much greater. She stated, "The Lord has given Sisera into your hand." She urged him forward by telling him his future, that they were about to finally defeat their greatest enemy, the one who had held them captive and oppressed them multiple times!

Although uncomfortable to admit, more of us probably relate to Barak than Deborah. More of us are more like the tentative child, feeling stretched and insecure, than the powerhouse leader charging into battle. What we have to remember is the truth Deborah declared to Barak.

She said, "Does not the Lord go out before you?" (Judg. 4:14 ESV) In other words, this isn't contingent on your strength. God only requires your faithfulness in obedience. He alone is responsible for the miracle.

Reflection

1. How would you compare Barak's response to your own?

2. In leadership, do you respond to someone's shortcomings like Deborah did?

3. Do you know someone you feel embodies the qualities of Deborah? Do you feel you do?

4. Scripture is the inerrant Word of God and all Scripture is God-breathed (2 Tim. 3:16 ESV). However, God did choose to relay His message through human authors. This is not a contradiction, but it also not something to ignore. Sometimes what is excluded actually emphasizes something very significant!

5. Consider a man feeling compelled to record, in heroic terms no less, the account of Deborah. His perspective would inherently be unbiased.

6. How is the time of Judges similar to the present day?

7. What are you proactively doing to avoid falling away from God?

Chapter 8

No R.E.S.P.E.C.T.

Leading the charge, the Israelites begin to descend upon the Canaanites in battle. They have to make the first move.

Down from Mount Tabor, Barak rides, swiftly navigating the treacherous terrain. His men rally behind him, but as they near the Canaanites, suddenly a great storm rolls in. The thunder, combined with the soundtrack of battle, is deafening—the cries, the grunting, the clamor of swords.

As the clouds burst above them, torrents of water burst through the face of the cliff. The rocky soil dislodges beneath the heavy chariot wheels, and the soldiers struggle to find their footing. Deborah watches as the chariots the Israelites had so greatly feared facing in battle became lodged in the rocks. One by one, they topple over, like a child's toy. Abandoned chariots now litter the battlefield.

Disoriented, some of the Canaanite soldiers become trapped, even crushed, under the weight of their chariots. Rather than carrying them to victory, their finely crafted war vehicles become the instruments of their own demise.

The mighty Canaanite army struggles to regain composure, but they weren't prepared for such fierce hand-to-hand combat. For every Israelite struck down, another tribe emerges to fight Sisera until every last man from Canaan is defeated.

In only a couple verses, we are told that "all the army of Sisera fell by the edge of the sword; not a man was left." Like Moses watching the Red Sea simultaneously free Israel and destroy their enemy, Deborah watched as water from heaven annihilated Israel's enemy and immobilized the Canaanite army. Now Sisera was the sole Canaanite survivor in a battle where the odds were severely against Israel, and Barak was hunting him down.

But here was where the consequences of Barak's earlier hesitation caught up with him. Remember verse 9? Deborah told Barak that he would not get the glory that day, but that "the mighty Sisera will be defeated by a woman."

Deborah's response to Barak was a clear indication of his subordinate role. As we are about find out, Deborah was not boasting that the credit will be hers, but instead that of another strategically placed woman.

Though some have relegated the roles of women in ancient Israel to purely homemakers, citing Deborah as the lone exception, archeological evidence is shedding light on women in pro-monarchist society, one that favors monarchy. This evidence suggests that women were involved in economic, judicial, religious, and legal affairs. The authors of Scripture would clearly not have been surprised by these discoveries, for as the story unfolds, we see another marginalized figure emerge as part of God's victorious plan.

Trembling and soaking wet, Sisera makes it off the battlefield and spots a lone woman outside her tent. Seeing her vulnerability, with no other man in sight, Sisera decides to make her home his hiding place. He knows he's being hunted, and his options are increasingly limited. Using a rug to conceal himself in Jael's tent, he asks her for a drink. Seeing his fatigue, she offers him some milk. Soothed by the milk, and weary from battle, he allows himself to rest. She's only a woman, after all. Not a real threat.

Jael watches as the man who has oppressed her people for so long lets down his guard and assumes she is incapable of action—a mistake that will cost him his life. She may be petite, but she is deceptively strong. Jael is a "tent-dweller," and what Sisera doesn't know is that she wields a hammer as effectively as any soldier wields a sword.

Unlike the accounts of male warriors, the Talmud is replete with salacious interpretations of exactly how Jael conned Sisera into falling asleep in her tent, with many suggesting a sexual encounter. It's a shocking twist to be sure, but to impugn Jael's character truly detracts from the point.

Perhaps she was a femme fatale, though for a book that never shies away from subjects like adultery, incest, rape, etc., the fact that it isn't made clear suggests that those details are not important. When Barak cowered, Deborah wasn't concerned. Why? Because she knew that victory wasn't contingent on man. She knew that if God said to go, they needed to move, and she makes it clear through her prophesy that God will accomplish His will with or without our participation.

Barak searches the entire battlefield for Sisera, tripping over fallen soldiers, their blood pooling in the puddles now flowing downhill from the storm. Adrenaline pulsing through him, he scarcely notices his own injuries.

When he cannot find Sisera on the battlefield, he makes his way through the tents. There Barak spots Jael standing outside, waving to him, curiously beckoning him over. Barak's heartbeat quickens, and as he draws closer, he prepares to draw his sword. Glancing down, he notices blood splattered on her face now streaked from raindrops, smeared on her dress, even covering her hands.

Jael calmly informs Barak, "Come . . . I will show you the man you seek."

Bewildered, he follows her gaze as she pulls back the tent curtain. With a tent peg jabbed straight through his temple, in a puddle of his own blood, lies the mighty Sisera.

We don't know the full circumstances around Sisera coming to Jael's tent. Some have theorized that her husband, an iron worker, had worked with him and actually forged weapons for the Canaanites. As noted before, some allude to an affair, but it's not explicitly stated; many of these theories emerge from material that has motive to diminish a woman's role.

What we do know is that Jael is fearless and accomplished what Barak could not. She slays the mighty Sisera and fulfills Deborah's prophesy—armed with only her household tools, a hammer, and a single tent peg.

"The earth trembled and the heavens dropped" (Judg. 4:4).

The battle was won! Although the credit for the victory did not lie with Barak, it truly was a victory for all Israelites, and the joy of that moment could not be contained. The euphoria was contagious! Though the ground was muddy, they danced. Though hoarse from shouting in battle, they sang. Barak and Deborah raised a song of victory, clapping like fools, deliriously happy. They glorified God that day, for His people were free!

When reading Scripture, it's easy to forget that it wasn't originally written in English. And it's not a few hundred years old, but thousands. Bible translators often title Judges 5 as "The Song of Deborah," and it was likely just that—an exclamation of praise after a hard-fought battle. Although many scholars believe it was composed at the time the events took place, the poem is not a hasty or uncontrolled expression.

"The Song of Deborah" is a complex and beautiful work. It tells a story, yet its form and eloquence stand alone. Even so, modern translations struggle to capture the original Hebrew. Although they can preserve the meaning, the beauty of the poem can feel clouded.

Echoing each other, Deborah and Barak are the victorious fulfillment of prophesy. One after another, the Israelites follow the clamor of Deborah's song—tribes emerging, joining in a celebration. It has been a long time since it has felt this way, since they had all come together as one family, set aside their disagreements, and truly embraced one another.

The women run and gather tambourines. They stomp their feet in the mud and shout so Israel's celebration could be heard for miles. As they dance and sing, tears of joy mixed with raindrops slide down their cheeks, glistening in the moonlight.

"Bless the Lord! Even the stars fought for us!" they say.

Poetry has a way of capturing the human experience more fully than the typical narrative. Though it may not flow like Shakespeare, the emotions and metaphors woven through Deborah's piece allow us a rare glimpse into the day of battle.

God used the very landscape and weather of the day, earthquake and rain, to assist the Israelites and deliver His people. Deborah honored others throughout the song. Most importantly, she honored God but also specific tribes who showed remarkable heroism.

Their bravery began before the battle with Sisera, when they turned back to God. Deborah spoke of tribal leaders who were called to rise up. She declared, "My heart is warmed by those in Israel called to command them, who offered themselves willingly to the people. Praise the Eternal One!" (Judg. 5:9)

She may have been their leader, but she made a point of

showcasing the community that worked together. Deborah knew the importance of unity. She may have been their prophet, judge, and military commander, but she was also a servant of God. God will always have the victory, but Deborah knew that His heart is for His people in the same way these leaders "offered themselves willingly to the people."

You may be asking, Why a song, though? I would argue it's the same reason that a song can be more meaningful than the phrase "I love you." A song can reach the heart in a way mere words fall short. Deborah was responsible for leading the people back to God and knew this required reaching their hearts, not just their heads.

"The stars themselves fought against them; from the heavens, the stars fought against Sisera" (Judg. 5:20 VOICE).

The joy of the moment of victory for Deborah was overwhelming. It wasn't about her status or being successful. Israel represented Yahweh. When the nations of the world looked at them, they looked for way of understanding a religion of only one deity. As long as Israel represented disorder and failure, other nations were free to assume their belief system was just as worthless.

The victory today would surely be a reason to reconsider.

The Israelites weren't the only nation struggling. In fact, due to an inept ruler coming into power in Egypt, surrounding nations were likewise suffering, as treaties of peace were being ignored and disorder was rampant.

In verse 8, Deborah referenced this and boldly contrasted the weakness of where they were prior to her rule to the victorious moment commemorated in her song. Picking up in verse 10 (VOICE), Deborah had just finished recalling the scattered and disorganized mess their kingdom had been, how there was not "a spear or shield to be found."

But her tone shifted dramatically in verse 10 and was almost taunting, as she sang, "Sing this song," and proceeded to deliver a triumphant story of Israel and declared the conquests of God. It's as if she was saying to all the nations who picked on them before, "Take that!"

But Deborah didn't just celebrate and honor the courageous leaders, she called out those who didn't rise up with them. She asked, "Why did you remain idle?" (v.16 VOICE). Deborah was presenting a challenge to the people: back your faith with action. She wasn't scolding the tribes to diminish them but to show them their potential, to empower them. In verse 21 (VOICE) she declared, "March forward, my soul, march on with strength!"

Most consider "The Song of Deborah" to be the oldest Hebrew poem. It is the only song of praise in the entire book of Judges.

"May those who love you be like the sun, rising and going forth in power" (Judg. 5:31 VOICE).

As the sun rose the next morning, Deborah couldn't help but think of Sisera's mother. War was an ugly reality, and in previous battles, the Israelites had not only witnessed the way the Canaanite soldiers took trophies, raped women, and enslaved those they defeated in battle, but they also had suffered and experienced these practices as well.

Sisera's mother had raised her son to believe those actions were right, which led to his death. His mother lived in a way that instead of bringing understanding, shrouds a mind in darkness.

But even as the Israelite soldiers gathered their dead to give them proper burial, judgment wasn't what Deborah felt in her heart; it was compassion. Deborah knew that she was not to take credit for the lives of her people or the peace that now reigned in Israel. Those who believe a lie are captive to it even in life, whereas Deborah knew clarity because she knew truth.

Deborah remains unquestionably the wise "mother" of Israel, admonishing her children and guiding them in wisdom. In the final portion of her song, we see her considering the mothers of the Canaanite soldiers slain, specifically Sisera's mother. While the Israelite soldiers were characterized as serving God, in Judges 5:30 (VOICE), the Canaanite soldiers are clearly motivated by "the spoils," which include "a girl or two given to every man."

Although it is clear that Deborah recognized his mother's pain, she also alludes to the blindness of Sisera's mother. While Deborah was given prophetic insight by God, Sisera's mother grasped in the dark for answers. Deborah sang about his mother imagining what he might bring her back from battle, an "embroidered cloth for my neck" (Judg. 5:30 VOICE), which obviously would never happen. It was pitiful and pathetic, as though her fancy scarf was nothing more than a decorative noose.

We begin to see that following God leads to understanding and insight, whereas those who chase after their own glory fall in darkness are deceived. Deborah finished her song praising God and giving Him full credit.

After verse 31, *The Voice* translation says, "After this victory, the people knew peace from war for 40 years." Deborah ruled for twenty, which only goes to show how far the wisdom with which she guided the people outlasted her. It also shows the fruit of following in the Law of Lord, which is what as a judge Deborah was charged with upholding. The inheritance of her wisdom, of following God's law, is peace.

Deborah may have been a brilliant military strategist, but teaching her people how to come back to God was without doubt her greatest accomplishment. If you grew up in church, you likely heard of Baal in Sunday School or heard the story of Daniel refusing to bow to the king, but the children's version of the story does not specify what worshiping such deities entailed.

Scripture makes clear that God is a "jealous God" (Ex. 20:5; Deut. 5:9; Josh. 24:19, and Nah. 1:2), and we are to have no other gods. However, when I hear people depict the God of the Old Testament as a warmonger, I can't help but cringe. God offers mercy to the societies that even prophets didn't want to see redeemed. Jonah, for example, objects to God's offer of mercy for Nineveh. But throughout the Old Testament, we often see entire nations spared. Not only that, but when we look at the cultic practices that these other gods involved, we are met with an unprecedented perversion.

Take a look at Leviticus where it says, "You shall not give any of your children to offer them to Molech, and so profane the name of your God: I am the LORD" (Lev. 18:21). This is followed by an extreme penalty in chapter 20, but what does it mean to "offer your children"?

Molech and Baal were both gods of prosperity and fertility. Shrines to these false gods were located in the Hinnom Valley just outside the city of Jerusalem, where refuse and trash were deposited. The belief was that sacrificing one's firstborn would ensure prosperity and/or fertility. Scholars conclude that fires were erected to superheat these statues, where the victim—a helpless child—was placed, and the playing of loud drums drowned out the infant's screams. No wonder this valley becomes the pictorial illustration of hell Jesus uses later.

Why is this horrific history important to know? Because not to fight this evil would be like saying Hitler should have been allowed to commit genocide. War is never pleasant, but evil is very real. Paul states in Ephesians 6:12, "For we do not wrestle against flesh and blood, but against the rulers, against the authorities, against the cosmic powers over this present darkness, against the spiritual forces of evil in the heavenly places."

Deborah was called to redeem Israel from oppression, but it

wasn't purely a physical oppression. Sure, archeology supports that a battle was waged between Sisera's army and the Israelite nation. Physical bodies fought each other, but the threat posed by this army was far more than earthly and territorial.

This battle was one of many in the Old Testament that was about keeping the Israelites from apostasy and spiritual death. Any push from society encouraging us to compromise is a spiritual attack. The Bible repeatedly calls us to live "set apart" and "holy lives" (2 Tim. 2:21; 1 Peter 2:5). Make no mistake, the enemy doesn't want this. We are still at war, and the question remains: Are we hesitating like Barak or charging forward like Deborah?

Reflection

1. We all have our desires, but in what areas of your life do you most struggle to surrender your will to God's?

2. Despite the incredible number of miracles and divine intervention God provides His people, Joshua, Judges, and 1 Samuel only include two expressions of praise. Both are composed by women: Deborah and Hannah. Consider why this might be.

3. Read Leviticus 20:1–5. Why do you think God's judgment is so much more extreme in the case of child sacrifice (even bystanders are held accountable) than, for example, murder?

4. What are some examples of modern-day spiritual warfare? How have you felt pressured to compromise in your own life?

5. Do you have friends in your life whom you can entrust to challenge you if you're not backing your faith with action?

6. I definitely grew up with the impression that the King James Version was what "serious Christians" used, but the KJV doesn't usually help me get into Scripture or understand it best. I like

reading different versions of the Bible for a better understanding of what is happening in a particular text. For poetic passages, I find *The Voice* translation helps me connect. For a more literal translation, I go to the *English Standard Version* (ESV). I highly recommend resources like *Blue Letter Bible* or the Bible App for comparing translations.

7. Who are the "tribal leaders" in your community of believers?

8. Although Jael slays the enemy and fulfills the prophecy, she is hardly honored for it. Do you find it hard to obey God when you won't necessarily be rewarded?

9. Sometimes we are called to fill in for a "Barak." Are you willing to answer when God calls you to pick up someone else's slack?

MARY DIDN'T KNOW

Chapter 9: Trial by Popular Opinion

"For nothing is impossible with God" (Luke 1:37).

Luke 1–20, 26–38

"And blessed am I as well, that the mother of my Lord has come to me!" (Luke 1:43 VOICE)

Luke 1:39–59; Matthew 1:18–24

"Gabriel appeared to her and said, "Greetings, favored woman! The Lord is with you!" (Luke 1:28)

Chapter 10: Staying the Course

"But his mother treasured all these things in her heart" (Luke 3:51 VOICE).

Luke 2:25–52; Hebrews 11:1

"Jesus' mother was standing next to his cross, along with her sister, Mary the wife of Clopas, and Mary Magdalene" (John 19:25).

John 19:13–30

"When I heard your greeting, the baby in my womb jumped for joy" (Luke 1:44).

Luke 1:39–45; Philippians 4:1-9

"He has brought down rulers from their thrones but has lifted up the humble" (Luke 1:52 NIV).

Chapter 9

Trial by Popular Opinion

"For nothing is impossible with God" (Luke 1:37).

Skepticism is defined as "doubt as to the truth of something," whereas faith, according to Paul, is the "confidence" of what we cannot see. The two are often at odds, and although faith is often described as blind, Scripture is clear that questions, when asked with the right motives, are good.

Scripture tells us to seek. Jesus said in Matthew 7:7, "Seek, and you will find." In Luke 24:45 we are told that Jesus "opened their [the disciples] minds to understand the Scriptures." God isn't playing games or trying to frustrate us in our ignorance. God requires us to act sometimes without being able to fully comprehend the whole picture, but our submission is in response to trusting that He does.

As humans, we often project human experiences onto God. We try to understand Him on our terms, perhaps viewing Him as an angry or absent father. Those negative feelings cause us to be skeptical of His plan. Remembering that God exists outside of our social structures, outside of even time and space, can be difficult. He doesn't share our limitations, yet He understands them. Trusting God isn't about knowing everything God does; it's about knowing Him.

Luke's Gospel clearly recognized this, and he addressed his account to a Roman official who was skeptical of Jesus. Luke wrote what scholars consider the most comprehensive of the gospel accounts, and just four verses in said, "I want you to know that you can fully rely on the things you have been taught about Jesus, God's Anointed One" (Luke 1:4 VOICE).

The temple was beautiful, the most prestigious place to work, and to be a priest was the most revered position for any Jew in the province of Judea!

There was a time when Zechariah's priestly duties were thrilling to him, the thought of being chosen a euphoric rush. It's not as though he didn't love God. He did, but he and Elizabeth were quite old, and life without children had grown rather routine.

They seemed to be constantly attending weddings and baby showers for their friends' children and grandchildren without ever knowing that experience for themselves, and their dutiful lives marched ever closer to the end.

Zechariah washes himself while the worshipers wait outside the temple, performing tasks that felt more habitual than holy. He is about to go into a sacred space, but his thoughts are distracted. It is as if he is going through the motions, forgetting the sacredness of his duties. As he carefully lights the incense and painstakingly follows the set guidelines for ritual, something very outside routine happens. Zechariah is not alone.

"Greetings," says the heavenly messenger in a resounding voice. Light surrounds him, as bright as a star, filling the temple.

Where had he come from? Zechariah drops the lighted stick in his hand, and the flame extinguishes as it hits the stone floor. The terror and awe of facing a supernatural being is overwhelming.

"I bring good news," the angel says, unphased by Zechariah's shock. "Your prayers have been answered! God will give you a son."

The angel goes on in great detail and without pause to tell

what a significant man of God Zechariah and Elizabeth's son will become, how he will "prepare the way for the Lord." The angel's speech seems to have no end, and Zechariah is becoming almost agitated as he listens in confusion and bewilderment. None of it makes any sense to him. It is like reading someone else's mail.

Finally, he impulsively blurts out, "But . . . I'm old!" Shaking his head, Zechariah's voice trails off. "And my wife . . . she's barren!"

The angel's serene face suddenly becomes solemn. He raises himself up and says in a forceful voice, "I am Gabriel."

Zechariah is instantly ashamed of his words, his face flushing red with shame. Gabriel continues, saying, "I stand in the very presence of God and have been sent today to tell you this good news."

Visibly trembling, Zechariah is unsure what the angel will say next.

"You will be silent until this day comes because of your lack of faith."

Suddenly his visitor vanished. Zechariah attempts to call out to him and ask questions but could make no sound, just as Gabriel had said.

Zechariah was unable to tell his wife about his encounter when he left the temple. Until the day of his son's birth, he could only write messages to her on tablets, like a middle-schooler passing notes in class. But he wasn't the only one who received unexpected news via a celestial postman.

Six months later, north of Jerusalem in a small town known today as "en-Nacirah," a teenage girl was betrothed to a carpenter named Joseph. They had grown up together and were looking forward to the celebration their families were planning.

Weddings are quite the event in Israeli culture, and in a small town they are especially elaborate because of the community's close-knit nature. Mary and Joseph were living according to the cultures and traditions of their families and dutifully upholding the laws of their faith. In short, their lives were ordinary. Then one morning, Mary was visited by an angel.

"Greetings! You are highly favored!"

Mary freezes. She has never seen an angel before and certainly doesn't understand what his "greeting" meant.

"Don't be afraid," says the angel, seeing the girl is terrified. "You have found favor with the Almighty."

Still, Mary can't speak.

The angel tells her she will give birth to a son, a Son of the Highest God! That He will be the Savior and rule the throne of David. Speechless, Mary attempts to absorb his words.

Then she feels the need to clarify something to this divine messenger. "I—I am a virgin. I've never been with a man."

The bizarre nature of this conversation with a celestial being briefly entered Mary's mind, but she has to know, how can this be possible?

The angel explains that this will be no ordinary conception—the baby will be born through the Holy Spirit. "It sounds impossible, but God wills it." Then he reminds her of her cousin, Elizabeth, who was also pregnant despite people thinking it was impossible.

"I am the Lord's servant," says Mary, eager to not seem unwilling. Yet silently Mary can't help wondering, *Of all people, why would God choose me?*

I think we all connect with the theme of an unlikely hero. Drawn in perhaps by the aspect of surprise, we tend to imagine ourselves in the role. But would we actually seize the opportunity if we came upon it?

In Luke 1, we have two people who are given similar news (one more outrageous than the other), and their responses are quite different. Zechariah was a priest, and at the moment he received his news, he was performing his priestly duties and burning incense while the worshipers had gathered outside.

This is where Gabriel, the angel of the Lord, entered and told him that he would have a son. Zechariah's response was one of doubt, and the angel was not pleased! Zechariah would have to wait several months before he could speak again.

Six months later, Gabriel visited Mary, a young unmarried Jewish girl whom we are given sparse details about. If we compare the two encounters, distinct similarities are present, but so are key differences. First, Gabriel had to reassure both of them they didn't need to be afraid. We can safely assume heavenly messengers are intimidating!

He also offered a blessing, telling Zechariah that his prayer would be answered and Mary that she was "highly favored." However, whereas Zechariah stated that granting his prayer request was impossible, due to his wife's and his age, Mary's question was, "How?"

These responses may seem similar, and they are, but noting the difference is imperative to understand what was going on with each of them. To not understand and ask a question is one thing, but to refute a statement altogether reveals lack of faith. Mary is young, unmarried, and certainly not a priest. Zechariah is elderly, well-educated, and in the middle of a sacred and holy duty. Yet it is Mary who responds, "I am the Lord's servant."

Mary would have no doubt faced severe scrutiny. Not only are we talking about "immaculate conception," but pregnant with the Messiah? The Jews were under an incredible weight of persecution by the Romans and anxiously waiting for a Savior whom they envisioned would ride in triumphantly to redeem them and establish an earthly rule.

They were imagining a supreme warrior to vanquish their foes! They were not expecting a vulnerable child, incapable of even feeding himself. Furthermore, Mary was young and not married. In the society of her day, no less credible a source could be found. More than likely, others would have assumed that she and Joseph had gotten pregnant and were making up the whole story of Gabriel and a Holy Spirit baby altogether.

Mary would have known all this. She would have known that she was about to face trial by popular opinion, with nothing but her word to defend her.

As soon as Gabriel left Mary, reality hit her. How was she going to explain this to her parents? To Joseph? To anyone? What if he didn't believe her? Would Joseph divorce her? How would she raise a child alone?

Mary could feel anxiety taking over, and she knew she couldn't stay and dwell on the what ifs. The angel had specifically mentioned Elizabeth, so she decided to go to her. Silently reminding herself that "His ways are higher," Mary began collecting her things. The trip was long, but she had made it before. It was still early. If she left now, she could make it before dark.

Luke provides no information on Joseph's decision not to divorce Mary, as was custom in what appeared a broken engagement. (This account is in Matthew.) Instead, Luke focuses on what Mary does next; he specifies what the person overlooked by society does:

"Mary immediately got up and hurried to the hill country, in the province of Judah, where her cousins Zechariah and Elizabeth lived" (Luke 1:39–40).

In other words, Mary sought out the one person she knew would encourage her faith. Mary is stiff and sweaty as she dismounts at Elizabeth's home. The journey has given her much time to reflect, but it was such a surreal turn of events, she can hardly put words to it.

As Mary approaches the door, she glances at her hands. Any exposed skin is filthy. She is quite a sight! The sand is caked on her face where her shawl had not covered, and she is so empty-handed that even her canteen is dry. With absolutely nothing to give her unsuspecting host, she walks through the familiar door.

Without hesitation, Elizabeth almost shouts with joy, "Blessed are you, Mary!" nearly echoing the words of the angel earlier. Then, Elizabeth says something Mary truly does not expect and prophetically announces, "And blessed am I that the mother of my Lord has come to me!"

Mary had not told anyone of her encounter but had instead come straight to Elizabeth. Hearing her cousin say what she could not have otherwise known was not only confirmation, but also indescribable comfort.

"God has noticed me!" Mary says.

She can't contain her joy. Elizabeth has confirmed that this was no dream! As daunting as it seemed for her life, Mary knows she is about to be a part of the redemptive story of Israel. She is about to experience the miraculous through herself.

Standing there, covered in the filth of her journey, Mary sings, "From generation to generation, God's lovingkindness endures for those who revere Him."

Sometimes our calling is going to seem outrageous to others. Sometimes even other Christians won't understand. But part of walking in faith is having the discernment to build relationships with others who will spur us on and encourage our faith.

Elizabeth did encourage Mary so much so that Mary burst into song. She sang, "All generations will call me blessed." Considering this was long before Jesus was born, let alone resurrected, Mary's faith was perhaps the single greatest feature of her character recorded by Luke.

Reflection

1. The word that Luke uses for treasured is the Greek word meaning "to keep continually or carefully." Consider how these moments would have looked after Jesus' crucifixion. What about after His resurrection?

2. Who do you turn to when facing a big decision or crisis of faith?

3. Are you the kind of friend who is likely to encourage someone in their faith, or do you find it difficult to trust and are more questioning?

4. Luke gives special attention to women in his gospel. He also shows remarkable consideration for the poor and those disadvantaged in society. Of the gospels, his account gives us perhaps the most depth in terms of Mary. What are some areas in your faith that you struggle to believe or have faith for?

5. How do you imagine you would have responded to Gabriel?

6. If we read further in Zechariah's story, you will find that the angel instructs him to name his son John. Names are extremely important in Scripture, and John's was more than just different from his father's, which would have been a very big deal in his day. Naming him John, or *yo-khaw-nawn*, which means "Jehovah bestowed," was a sign of Zechariah's obedience, of surrendering to the will of God. When Zechariah declares John's name, his voice is restored.

Chapter 10

Staying the Course

"But his mother treasured all these things in her heart" (Luke 3:51 VOICE).

Mary and Joseph never missed the Passover festivities. Their families all joined together and caravanned to Jerusalem. It was a celebration! This party lasted several days. People they rarely got to see would be there, and everyone traveled together as a procession; the cousins played while the adults got caught up.

But in the year Jesus was born, a man named Simeon approaches them. Taking Jesus in his arms, he says, "Now, Lord and King, you can let me, your humble servant, die in peace!"

Mary is confused by his abrupt greeting but does not interrupt.

"You promised I would see Your light—Your freedom. He is Your light!"

Mary and Joseph exchange glances but are unsure how to respond. Simeon is clearly not speaking to them but to their baby.

Then he turns, and looking at them both, says, "Listen, this child will make many in Israel rise and fall. In the end, he will lay bare the secret thoughts of many hearts." Looking sorrowfully at Mary, Simeon says, "And a sword will pierce even your own soul, Mary."

Before either could ask any questions, Anna rushes over. At eighty-four years old, she is known for her incredibly devout faith. When she sees Jesus, she shouts with joy, "Thanks be to God for the rescue of Israel!" Anna proclaims Jesus to be the Messiah, and Mary and Joseph watch in silent wonder and awe.

Have you ever had a prayer request that felt as if it would never be answered? Was it something that was so important you couldn't let it go, but you wondered or maybe even doubted you would ever get an answer? Maybe it's so great a request that it makes it difficult to keep going, keep believing, which makes you feel alone.

Many people in Mary's story were waiting on an unfulfilled promise. In chapter 2, Anna and Simeon approached Mary regarding Jesus. Anna was elderly, and although we aren't given an exact age for Simeon, he declared that now he had finally seen the fulfillment of God's promise, he could "die in peace."

It's a beautiful scene, but one can't help but wonder what it must have been like waiting for so long. Mary herself was waiting, remaining faithful, even when she could not understand. Throughout Jesus' life, the gospels repeatedly record her confusion (and the perplexity of other followers), yet she remained steadfastly committed. We catch a glimpse of when Luke recounted a story from Jesus' childhood.

One year during the Passover festivities, when Jesus is about twelve, the time had come to return to Nazareth. Mary and Joseph tell the kids. By now they all know the routine and begin the trek as usual, the large caravan of aunts, uncles, and cousins all together. About a day into their journey home, Mary and Joseph realize they haven't seen one of their sons in a while.

After much fruitless inquiry, they rush back to Jerusalem, and at this point, they are frantically searching. Finally, they go to the temple where they are stunned to find him in reflective conversation with the religious teachers. His ease in contrast to their beleaguered panic pushes Mary over the edge.

In frustration, she says, "Son, we have been so worried! For three days, we looked everywhere for you!"

Jesus looks almost confused as He calmly says, "Didn't you know I would be in my Father's house?"

Neither Mary nor Joseph know what He means. Neither know what to say, but Mary continues to store up these memories in her heart, believing they will one day make sense.

When Mary and Joseph thought they'd lost Jesus, and He stated that He was "in my Father's house," Scripture says that Mary and Joseph did not understand. Typically, the parents were the ones explaining to the children. Can you imagine feeling as though your preteen son knows more than you?

Even as a boy, Jesus was God. Yet, rather than be annoyed, Scripture says that Mary "treasured all these things in her heart." They may only be memories, anecdotes of Jesus' childhood, but just like individual puzzle pieces work together to form the whole picture, these isolated memories are not insignificant. Mary knew this and believed that although now she didn't understand, she would. This is one of the hardest practices of faith, but it is fundamental: believing in what we cannot see.

As we read further in the Bible, and in Mary's story, we realize the arrival of Jesus wasn't only a surprise to her, but to the people of Israel. Thousands of years of expectation and longing was building toward His grand entrance, but the Jews had endured four hundred years of silence. Not one prophecy between Malachi and John the Baptist announced Christ's birth.

Then their Messiah arrives in the most unexpected way. The oppressed Jews were quite familiar with war and were confidently expecting a valiant king riding in and defeating all their enemies. They instead received a helpless baby born to an unremarkable, unmarried virgin teenager. Obviously, God chose this unremarkable girl and saw something very significant in her. But by the standards of her day, Mary was not distinguished by any circumstances that would merit special attention—except for Jesus.

The reception at the wedding in Cana is a disaster. They are out of wine! The wedding festivities are well underway, but the wine has run out. Humiliation is imminent. Mary whispers the situation to Jesus, who makes it clear that this was not His appointed task on earth. But Mary knows her son, so she subsequently turns to the servants and says, "Do whatever He tells you."

Jesus smiles knowingly at His mother. He knows she will insist. Jesus had observed six thirty-gallon stone water jugs by the door earlier—the kind they used for Jewish ceremonial purification—and tells them to fill them with water.

The servants do what Jesus says.

"Fill a cup and give it to the headwaiter."

They all glance nervously at one another. Give the headwaiter a cup of water? Then one servant shrugs and obediently fills a cup. Why not?

When the headwaiter tastes it, he immediately rushes to the host, saying, "Why would you save the best wine for last?"

We could unpack so much in this story, but I want to point out how relatively insignificant this miracle is. It's wine. No lives are at stake here! No risk of injury, except for some hurt pride on behalf of the host. Yet, Mary already knows that Jesus cares even about the little things.

Teenage motherhood by supernatural intervention could not have been how Mary envisioned her life or family. As incredible as it may appear for us who know the end, Mary didn't. Yet she appears repeatedly throughout Jesus' life and ministry.

She is present in John 2—the first of many miracles she would witness—and her actions tell us that she remained faithful when it would have been easy to recede into the background. It would have been easy to let her expectations interfere with her understanding the Savior before her.

We do this ourselves, don't we? We expect our lives, our jobs, and our families to look a certain way; and when they don't, it can be easy to assume that we didn't make the special list. Or we're not highly favored. We start looking for a way to make appearances match our expectations, and we settle for the imitation.

Speaking from personal experience, insecurity is not an attractive quality. We need to take a note from Mary's book and choose to believe in God's promises every day until we experience them.

"We also celebrate in seasons of suffering because we know that when we suffer we develop endurance, which shapes our characters. When our characters are refined, we learn what it means to hope and anticipate God's goodness" (Romans 5:3 VOICE).

I once heard a preacher give the analogy that your belief in gravity changes when you're standing on a ladder. He then proceeded to climb precariously high—I was uncomfortable watching him—and I found the simplicity so beautiful. Faith in God is the same way, but how comfortable are you?

Jesus is standing on a cliff face, and behind Him is Mount Tabor, the very same mountain on which the prophetess Deborah had led the Israelites to victory against Sisera and the Canaanite army.

Jesus is speaking to friends and those who have known Him since He was a boy, people who know the significance of the mountain. Jesus boldly declares the words of Isaiah: "In short, the

Spirit is upon me to proclaim that now is the time." In their familiarity, however, they resent Him. When He continues to tell them that the sacred words of Scripture are being fulfilled through Him, they become enraged.

Jealously a man grabs Him by His collar, saying, "Who do you think you are?"

Another angrily shoves Him; some are holding large rocks in their hands. They begin to push Him until He is standing on the very edge of the cliff. The Savior they had desired for centuries, they are now prepared to kill.

Mary chose to be present throughout Jesus' ministry, which we might mistakenly liken to helping at our local church; however, this was a far more radical calling. Jesus was preaching a message that was enraging many of the leaders Mary would have grown up following. He was not simply stirring up commotion or gossip but anger to the point they attempted to murder Him.

The previous scene is from Luke, and it's one of many examples of an angry mob threatening to stone, or in this instance, push Jesus over the edge of a steep and rocky hill. It's one of many times that Scripture says He escaped because "his time had not yet come" (John 7:30; 8:20).

Imagine for a moment being His mother, knowing what the angel told you before His birth but trying to defend His message to your friends and family—a message that you were struggling to understand. We aren't given details of Jesus' home life, we aren't told specifically who Mary trusted or confided in, but we continually see her by Jesus' side.

We always see her with others who were making the choice to follow Him. This is significant because it is our example of how to stay faithful, even when life doesn't make any sense. For Mary it would become even more confusing and more painful to stay close to Jesus. The crowds were becoming increasingly angry, the officials more determined to silence Him. The threat of death was closing in around Jesus, and Mary and His followers knew it.

When Jesus fell, she couldn't pick Him up. When He cried, she couldn't soothe His pain.

The crowd either jeered or were there to witness the spectacle. They were pleased to watch Him suffer. She could hear the soldiers casting lots for His clothing, her son now stripped of the last shred of His dignity.

They saw a man; Mary saw her baby. Clinging to John's arm, she had no strength left to stand.

"Dear woman," Jesus lovingly says.

Through her tears she looks up at Him. Blood is running down His face as He struggles for every agonizing breath.

"This is your son," He says, nodding toward John, "and this," He says, looking at John, "is your mother."

His mother, the one who witnessed His first breath is now witnessing His last.

Mary was present even at His crucifixion. She watched as her son was tortured and murdered, knowing the injustice of it, knowing His death was for them. John records a tender moment just before Jesus breathes His last breath. John 19:28 says, "Jesus knew now that His work had been accomplished and the Hebrew Scriptures were being fulfilled."

Jesus knew—not Mary, not John. Only Jesus. And yet, Mary remained faithfully present.

Sometimes I think it's easy for us to look at who we might consider giants of the faith and almost exclude ourselves as though we could never measure up. Mary was human. She was no different from you or me. She was further up the ladder—not because she was born that way, but because she chose to climb. She chose to keep going, even when she didn't understand. If she is a giant of faith, it's because she climbed that high.

When the crowds had faded at Golgotha, only a few remained. Mary was one of the few, watching through swollen eyes as her son was taken off His cross. A wealthy man from Arimathea had offered Jesus a brand-new tomb, a gesture of love.

Mary and a group of women followed as the men laid Him behind cut stone to rest. Although Pilate's men were posted to guard the tomb for fear someone would steal Jesus' body, the women prepared to return after the Sabbath and give Him proper burial ointments. They would honor the Hebrew Scriptures, resting on the Sabbath, and then somehow get around the Roman centurions guarding their Lord's tomb.

They didn't leave Him, not even in death.

If we look at Mary's story, testimony and sharing faith has been an ever-present theme from the beginning. The very first thing she does after Gabriel tells her about Jesus is to tell Elizabeth. The very first words from her at Jesus' first miracle are "Do whatever He tells you," which is a declaration of faith on her part, knowing that He had the answers. And her first response to His resurrection was to go tell the good news, initially to fellow believers and then the whole world.

As we have seen, Mary did not live in a society that revered women. She did not always understand, and her faith would have been challenged daily. Mary needed community. The ability to share our testimony is a gift that is meant to encourage others.

Consider Paul's words in Philippians 4. He talks about those who have kept his faith strong and about guarding our hearts and minds. In verse 9 he gives us a practical way of doing so: "Finally, brothers, whatever is true, whatever is honorable, whatever is just, whatever is pure, whatever is lovely, whatever is commendable, if there is any excellence, if there is anything worthy of praise, think about these things."

Sometimes our testimony feels so personal we would rather keep it to ourselves, but this is not what Scripture tells us to do. Your conversion and all that God has done in your life so far may have taken place in the past, but it shouldn't stay there. It's meant to be shared!

When we, like Paul, make a point of rallying together around what is true, praiseworthy, and honorable, our hearts and minds will be guarded by God's peace.

It was still dark, and the ground is wet with dew. The baskets are heavy as the women make their way silently to Jesus' tomb. Mary tries to think of a way to persuade the guards to let them pass, but nothing comes to mind.

She is still numb from last Friday, is unable to cry anymore, and unable to feel much of anything. It likely doesn't matter anyway because her speech will undoubtedly fall on deaf ears. The Romans rarely listened to reason, and even less likely coming from a woman.

As they approach, they realize the stone was askew. In horror, Mary drops her basket, glasses of precious oils smashing together as they hit the ground. The room is dark, but Mary begins desperately groping about. She can't find her son!

Just then, two men appear, their clothes gleaming like lightning! The women fall down. One shrieks, and the scream echoes throughout the empty tomb. They are trembling.

In chorus, the two men ask, "Why do you look for the living among the dead?"

Mary hesitantly looks up, hope stirring within her. "Living?"

"Don't you remember? He told you He must be crucified, and then on the third day He must rise!"

Suddenly it all makes sense. The women shout and hug one another. He is alive! Their shared experience is made all the more powerful as they rejoice together.

There's something to be said about a party. Whether a graduation or a pre-game tailgate, celebration just isn't quite as motivating alone. But when you're in a group, it's a rally! One of my favorite pictures of my youngest daughter was taken the day her cousin was born. Though only two years old, and not able to fully comprehend the significance of a child being born, her joy is overflowing as she grabs his sister in an embrace. It's as though she's congratulating her on her new brother, and the joy is contagious!

If we go back to the beginning of Mary's story, we find a similar celebration. Mary's journey to Elizabeth was full of purpose, and her cousin's joyous reception stirs her faith into powerful praise. Though likely connected to what Gabriel told her regarding her cousin, Mary's journey to Elizabeth also suggests a bond and an existing relationship that was strong enough for her to feel confident in her cousin's reaction.

When Elizabeth greets her, Mary's baby "leapt in her womb"! Scripture also says that Elizabeth "was filled with the Holy Spirit." Can you imagine how full the presence of God felt as these two women—one carrying Jesus incarnate and the other filled with the Holy Spirit—must have been? Later Paul goes on to write about the power of fellowship. In Ecclesiastes 4:9 he says, "Two are better than one." Community is in our best interest.

Mary recognized this. The verses in Luke 1:46–55 are referred to as Mary's Song of Praise. The words are prophetic and are by no means single-minded. She praises God, and although she mentioned what Jesus did for her, the majority of her song speaks to the economic, political, and social ways that God was about to move through the Messiah. The people of Mary's day would have readily understood what she was talking about, as daily life under Roman rule would have been a constant reminder that they were not free.

Mary referred to Old Testament prophecies being fulfilled, but she also clearly understood that this was not how anyone foresaw it happening. In verse 51 she said, "The proud in mind and heart God has sent away in disarray." She recognized that the journey and the assignment she had accepted contradicted popular thought among her people.

Yet her song emphatically declared, "My spirit rejoices in God my Savior." Most people won't understand what we believe, but we should never let that hold us back from sharing with others or praising God amidst an overwhelming assignment.

The women rushed back to the disciples. Mary was almost overcome as she recalled that moment with Elizabeth, the joy overflowing that led to her song. She recalled so many instances throughout Jesus' childhood that had made no sense at the time, but she had stored them up and now they were perfectly clear. Jesus had humbled the proud and used the unlikely to confound those who considered themselves wise. The words of the angel echoed in her ears: "His kingdom will never end." Not even death could hold Him down!

When they reach the upper room where the disciples are hiding in fear for their lives, the women begin exclaiming what they had seen! The men look on in disbelief. "Lies!" They respond angrily. They do not believe a word.

The women insist, telling them about the angels and how they had repeated Jesus' words, but the men all dismiss them.

Then, Peter jumps up and runs to the tomb. When he finds it empty, he still does not believe the women's story.

An argument has been made that the women of the New Testament, purportedly the first to bear witness to Jesus' resurrection, went to the wrong tomb. It seems to me a thinly veiled insult. The women have such poor navigation skills that they went to the wrong tomb? Really?

However, given the culture of the time, the sheer fact that they are credited as the first witnesses (not to mention, the first to believe in Jesus' resurrection) is surprising, to say the least. Male chauvinism was rampant in ancient society, which was not exclusive to Judean culture.

Women were considered second-class citizens at best. Even the female mythological gods were second class. The most powerful of the ancient Greek goddesses, Athena, was said to be merely a figment of Zeus' mind. The legend states that she "popped out of his head"! In other words, her autonomy was limited to the confines of his imagination, which speaks to the inhibited lives of the women in this ancient Roman society.

But this bias, rather than bolstering men's opinions, actually lends credibility to the women's claims. Consider the men compiling the Gospels: Would they have wanted to admit that they were hiding in an upper room from the Jewish leaders while the women were boldly going to honor Jesus at His resting place? Remember that this tomb was guarded, Pilates' orders, to prevent anyone from spreading rumors about the divinity of Jesus.

For a society that so highly regards manliness, this seems to suggest a severe role-reversal! If the author wanted to fabricate an account, he would certainly have chosen a more credible kingpin. Besides, according to rabbinic law, the women's testimony was no more valuable legally than that of a criminal. A woman was rarely, if ever, present in court because why bother? No one was going to believe a woman.

Regardless, the women did just as Jesus told them and testify! Others likely scoffed at their story, but they didn't keep silent and were in fact the first evangelists. Matthew made a point of show-casing Mary's example: "When the disciples saw Jesus there, many of them fell down and worshiped, as Mary and the other Mary had done." At the head of the Great Commission were the women—disregarding society's perception of them and faithfully declaring their testimony. More than their reputations, they risked nothing less than their lives.

Paul wrote to the church of Corinth: "God chose the foolish in the world to shame the wise." Mary was certainly a most unex-pected way for the Messiah to enter the world, but she was exactly the way God chose. A baby was the most unexpected form, but that is exactly how our Savior came to us. The women of Jesus' day were the most unlikely choice for the first evangelists, but that is precisely whom God chose.

Mary carried Jesus in His incarnate form, but you and I carry His presence because of His Holy Spirit; that presence has the same power to change the world.

Reflection

1. Do you praise God on a daily basis, or does your worship remain a church activity?

2. Mary's journey to Elizabeth was no casual stroll. The distance between their two villages is roughly one hundred miles. Although her betrothed would likely have arranged a caravan for her to make the journey, it still required considerable effort and, for an expectant mother, would have been quite taxing. Where do you go to be encouraged in your faith?

3. Who do share your testimony and what God is doing in your life with?

4. Most scholars believe Philippians was written while Paul was under house arrest in Rome, during the reign of Nero, one of the most violent persecutors of Christianity. Paul knew he was risking his life by writing the churches and preaching the gospel, yet he persists. He knew what it meant to "guard you heart and mind," and we can be assured that his overflow of gratitude to those who had encouraged him along the way was genuine.

5. Questions are good. What are some questions you're wrestling with today?

6. Do you have a hard time believing that you are favored of God? Commit to reading at least a verse of Scripture every time you go on social media. Let His voice be louder than society's.

7. Only a couple people in the Bible are distinguished by God as "highly favored." One other, besides Mary, is Moses. In Exodus 33:17, God says to Moses, "This very thing that you have spoken I will do, for you have found favor in my sight, and I know you by name."

8. The word choice of *theoreo* in Greek, meaning "to perceive," represents more than just seeing. If the gospel was only suggesting physical sight, the word *horao* would be a more appropriate word choice. Mark 16:4 suggests that the women understood what had happened when they saw the stone rolled away and an empty tomb, something that required the incarnate person of Jesus opening their minds in order for the men to believe.

YOU DON'T KNOW MY NAME

Chapter 11: I Have Issues

"And yet you say, "Who touched me?" (Mark 5:31).

The good shepherd leaves the many for the one.

"Power has gone out from me" (Luke 8:46).

Chapter 12: The Miracle Is Not the Message

"Do not fear, only believe" (Mark 5:35).

"Your faith has healed you" (Luke 8:48).

Faith for others, even when it looks impossible.

Chapter 11

I Have Issues

Anyone who lived through the pandemic knows what it is to feel isolated. Coming out of quarantine, even for introverts, there was a very real longing for human interaction—for personal touch. And it wasn't just the lack of haircuts that plagued us all. I can remember laughing with friends about how we all felt socially awkward and way too eager for an actual hug or face-to-face, rather than Facetime conversation.

The ancient Israelites were what is known as a "collectivist culture." In a collectivist culture, the community is given priority, and decisions that in modern western society we might consider the right of the individual are made by the group. Community is everything, and for the Israelites, there are times when this is even reflected in their laws, such as we see in the book of Leviticus.

Take for example the fact that, next to death, was the punishment of exile. To be exiled was in some ways worse, for everything you were, was viewed in light of the community. To be exiled was to lose your very identity, to become nothing.

Much of the Old Testament, including Leviticus, however, is difficult to read, and many of us, if we're honest, would say we skim-read or skip it altogether. It's dense to be sure, and full of laws and procedures. But it's also a valuable tool for understanding the worldviews and mindsets of ancient Israelites. In order to understand the motives of the characters throughout the Bible, it is necessary to view them in this light.

Many of the laws governing Jewish society revolved around purity—what is ritually impure and what is morally impure. Ritual impurity was not viewed as a moral failure. Things that were normal and natural made you ritually impure; things that were unavoidable such as skin diseases or contact with mold or a dead body would make a person "unclean." But these things were also reminders of our fallen state, reminders that humanity was no longer in the garden of Eden.

In the case of ritual impurity, a person was required to quarantine, and anyone who touched that person would likewise be considered unclean. In the synoptic gospels we read about a woman who has been living in such a condition for twelve years—far beyond the two weeks an individual would normally be estranged from society. She is unnamed, and her story is a mere few verses long, yet she is renowned for her faith.

Another birthday alone. Another day spent cleaning blood. So many physicians, so many painful treatments, and so far, none could heal her. She had spent the last of her wealth, desperate to have her life back, but she remained in isolation. Her life was void of everything but the memory of what used to be.

Some blamed her; they said God was judging her for an unconfessed sin. Some speculated that the sins of her parents were being visited on her. She knew this made it easier for them. Even her "pity visits" were becoming scarce, and anyone who dared touch her is immediately declared ceremonially unclean. And the bleeding only kept getting worse. She is out of options and soon would be out of time.

Luke documents the woman with the issue of blood in his gospel, and as a physician himself, lends considerable weight to her story. He says she "had suffered a great deal." Although likely dealing with a hemorrhage, scholars debate where exactly the bleeding was occurring. Due to the discretion of the gospel writers, the general consensus is that it was a menstrual bleeding—she had been having her period for twelve years. The fact that her bleeding was becoming worse suggests she was terminally ill.

She was estranged from people at home and would not have been allowed in the temple to worship God. Her estrangement would undoubtedly have impacted her spiritually, causing her to question His plan for her. His love for her.

The Synoptic Gospels—Matthew, Mark, and Luke—all record two significant events leading up to our encounter with the hemorrhagic woman. Before moving forward with her account, let's consider what the author wanted us to recognize through each narrative.

The first is a story that, if you grew up going to Sunday School, you've probably heard many times. Basically, the disciples were with Jesus on the Sea of Galilee, and Jesus fell asleep on the boat. A violent storm rolled in, and the disciples are so afraid that they woke Jesus up, saying, "We're going to drown!"

Now, these men were no amateur fishermen. The position of the Sea of Galilee is such that a sudden storm can produce waves in excess of seven feet high. The men had good reason to be frightened, but if you've read the story, you know that Jesus spoke to the wind and water, and everything instantly became calm. Mere words brought the natural world into submission. Jesus then said something that each of the gospels record. He rebuked the disciples for their fear, asking, "Where is your faith?"

Once the disciples get across the lake, the authors record a second significant event. As soon as Jesus stepped ashore, they were greeted by something far more frightening than a storm: a naked demoniac who lived in tombs. The demon, in fact, drove the man to isolation.

Though the people of his village had tried to restrain him by binding him with chains, the demon compelled him to break the chains and cut himself with rocks. This same demon no human can subdue, however, is clearly terrified of Jesus and begs Him for mercy.

When Jesus cast the demon out of him, we find out that there are actually many demons—they answer as "Legion," which is a Roman term, meaning an army of about six thousand. The disciples watch as Jesus proves that He has authority over all of them. First the natural, then the supernatural world bow to Him.

All three authors included these events before they referred to the hemorrhagic woman. All three follow her account with Jesus, sending out His twelve disciples to teach and heal. This is an important parallel that can be easy to miss. These are not disconnected stories that happen to be in the same book, but rather a carefully woven narrative. Each story provides a fuller depth of understanding and helps us to grasp what Jesus was really telling us.

There was so much commotion regarding Jesus. The religious leaders despised Him, claiming His message was nothing short of sacrilegious. The Son of God—how dare He claim divinity? Furthermore, He was healing on the Sabbath and associating with sinners—even the pagan Samaritans!

But the more the woman with the issue of blood listened, the more she believed. Isolation meant considerable time on her hands, and she had become particularly fixated on the words of the prophet Isaiah, words she knew Jesus claimed to fulfill. She had heard them in the temple her whole life, committing to memory as much as she could. Watching the way Jesus was treated, she couldn't help but recall them: "He was despised and rejected by mankind, a man of suffering . . . he was despised."

They hated him, many even threatening to kill Him, yet He continued to help people.

"He took up our pain and bore our suffering, yet we considered him punished by God."

Alone, with only her thoughts, the woman couldn't help but feel a stirring in her spirit—a stir of hope. Jesus was healing people with leprosy, and driving out demons. Surely He could heal her too! But how could she reach Him?

We aren't given many details in the gospels on what this woman's daily life would have consisted of because the original audience would have been well aware. Ostracized from her people, having spent all she had, with her symptoms growing increasingly worse, her future would have loomed darkly ahead.

The gospels make clear that, once privileged, she became destitute, so she was likely living reliant on the charity of others. Yet somehow, this woman had managed to keep her faith in God and recognize that Jesus was her answer. It would have been easy to feel trapped and give up, but she doesn't. Instead, she rallies. Twelve years a terminal patient, she refuses to surrender the only thing she has left—her faith.

The crowd is massive and so focused on Jesus that they scarcely notice her. As they press in to see Jesus, she whispers apologies to those now unclean for coming into contact with her. She feels like some kind of bacteria—infecting an unbeknownst crowd, while simultaneously longing just to be held. If she could just get to Jesus. Just the hem of His robe would be enough!

Her head throbs, and the dizziness is becoming acute. Her vision is blurring, and her legs feel numb. Every step is sheer agony.

As we read in both Mark and Luke, she approached Jesus

while He was on the way to help a man named Jairus. Jairus has approached Jesus regarding his twelve-year-old daughter. She was very ill, unresponsive, and possibly already dead. Jairus was clearly distraught. We are told in both gospel accounts that Jairus was a synagogue leader, which is surprising considering the controversy surrounding Jesus. A man in his position, Jairus would have known thoroughly the arguments against Jesus' teaching and was now begging for His help.

Jairus even asked for His healing touch, saying, "Come and put your hand on her and she will live" (Matt. 9:18). Considering Jesus has just come from healing a demon-possessed non-Jew, we can clearly see that this man was willing to risk every bit of his elite status because of his faith in Christ. Jesus did not delay. He immediately proceeds to follow Jairus to his home, but before he gets there, Jesus was unexpectedly interrupted.

Bumping into people, pushing her way forward, she is quickly becoming overwhelmed with fatigue. Suddenly a man wearing fine linen clips her shoulder and sends her stumbling forward. As she hits the ground, someone behind her yells, "Hey!" and another, "Watch out!"

The brick pavement is hot from the afternoon sun. She scrapes her palms, her knees are raw, and her arms and legs are now covered in bruises. Every time she tries to get up, someone else knocks her down. As she looks behind her, she sees a trail of blood smeared by the heavy foot traffic, and a flush of red-hot embarrassment shoots through her.

Her head is spinning as she tries to slow her pounding heart-rate.

"Just breathe," she tells herself. "You can do this. You just need to touch Him."

Stumbling, crawling, desperately seeking, she makes her way

through the crowd. Then, extending herself as far as she can, she gingerly grasps the hem of his robe.

Reflection

1. Have you ever prayed for healing?

2. What's the longest you've waited for a prayer to be answered?

3. How did the wait affect you spiritually?

4. Does the wait make you question God's plan?

5. The woman's miracle happens after she had reached the end of herself—after she had lost everything. Likewise, Jairus' daughter had lost everything, even her life. Which begs the question: In similar circumstances, would our faith remain intact?

6. What kind of obstacles are in your way to get to Jesus?

7. Does the theme of touch in the woman's story make you nervous? Do you cringe at the thought of laying hands on a sick person for healing?

Chapter 12

The Miracle Is Not the Message

Stopping abruptly, Jesus asks, "Who touched me?"

The disciples look at Him—was He joking? Who isn't touching Him right now would be easier to answer. The crowd is pressing in on all sides, even the disciples are feeling claustrophobic. Confused, they glance around. Then shrugging, they answer, "What do You mean? All these people are pressing against You."

"I felt power leave me," Jesus calmly responds, still scanning the crowd for who had touched Him. The disciples exchange glances and begin to scan the crowd, unsure of what they are looking for, but imitating Christ.

A couple moments pass, the crowd noise seems a distant hum, and the suspended silence feels like years. The woman realizes she will not go unnoticed today. After twelve years of isolation, of no physical touch with scarcely any visitors to witness her shame, she is now having to tell her story to this entire crowd of people.

"It was me," she almost whispers, immediately falling at his feet. "I touched you."

People immediately begin whispering—this is entirely inappropriate. She had crossed the line of decency. How dare she touch Jesus!

But instead of begrudging her boldness, Jesus smiles at her as she continues.

"For twelve years I have suffered, unable to be cured by any doctor, but the instant I touched Your robe, I was healed!"

"Daughter," Jesus says, stooping down to look her in the face, "your faith has healed you."

Some have relegated her to no more than a superstitious woman. After all, in the ancient world, healing was often equated with magic. Additionally, she touched His clothing, and garments were heavily symbolic. Jesus' response to her is significant: "Daughter, your faith has healed you."

Jesus doesn't even credit Himself or make mention of His authority. He directly credits her faith. Certainly it was His power that healed her, but Jesus directly ties her healing to the faith she held onto. Paul's letter to the church at Galatia puts it this way:

"Miracle after miracle has occurred right before your eyes in this community, so tell me: did all this happen because you have kept certain provisions of God's law, or was it because you heard the gospel and accepted it by faith?"

Paul goes on to say that even Abraham wasn't justified by law, but his faith was counted as righteousness. This would have certainly upset many Jews! At that time in history, unity among the Jewish people was less about theology and more about a way of life.

Rituals and law were the defining aspects of Judaism, not faith. People knew you were a Jew by what you ate or didn't eat, by your observance of the Sabbath or the feast of Passover. These things distinguished you from the Gentiles, and the more devout you were or the more rigid you were in your ritual practices, the better a Jew you were.

Hundreds of years of captivity had resulted in several different groups of Jews, and each had their own priorities and their own emphases when reading the Bible. There were the Pharisees, the Sadducees, the Essenes, and so on, and what united them wasn't necessarily common doctrine since over the years, they had essentially grown apart in their interpretations of the sacred Word. They argued over those differences at length, but what they agreed on were the rituals and the visible demonstrations of their religion.

What Jesus was proposing would have leveled the playing field because no longer would there be a scalable level of devoutness and ritual adherence; there would be a kingdom of faith, one where all were welcome—even the unclean.

The gospel accounts go on to emphasize this point, for even as Jesus was speaking, we read that some of those who were waiting for Him at Jairus' house rush out to tell Him that Jairus' daughter had died. The connection between these events can easily be missed. Look at what Scripture says.

While Jesus was still speaking to her, some people rush out of Jairus' home to tell him that his daughter has already died—that he was too late and only wasting Jesus' time. They told him, glancing over his shoulder at Jesus, "Don't bother the teacher anymore."

Jairus' heart drops, tears immediately brimming in his eyes. It is as though everything has stopped; everything is dark. He feels completely numb, empty. His heart is only a hollow ache inside his chest. His baby girl, how could she be gone?

Overhearing what they said, Jesus looks at Jairus, saying, "Don't be afraid, just believe."

Rubbing the tears off his face with his sleeve and trying to appear strong, Jairus avoids the teacher's gaze and instead looks down at the woman. Looking into her eyes, her faith stirs something like hope within him. It is as though she is silently willing him a portion of her faith.

Jesus healed her when no one else could. Could Jesus raise his daughter as well?

Jairus summons all his courage as he walks beside the teacher to his home, commanding himself to keep walking. His sandals feel heavier with every step, his heart pounding in his chest, and his brow furrowed in determination as they drew near.

When they arrive, it was as if the oxygen has left the room. People are weeping and huddling together, holding one another. They stare as he and Jesus approach.

Softly, Jesus assures those gathered, "Don't cry." He calmly and confidently says, "She's only sleeping. Don't be afraid."

Jairus can hear the snickering, some outright laughing and shaking their heads. "As if we couldn't tell the difference," someone says. Jesus turns to one of the relatives and asks him to escort the crowd out. The man does so at once, and as they leave, it feels as if a weight has been lifted. Jairus proceeds to take Jesus to his daughter's bedside.

"*Talitha koum!*" Jesus commanded.

Jairus watches as his daughter immediately stands up and begins walking about as if she had never been sick.

The gospel writers saw clear connections between these two accounts. Jairus' daughter was twelve years old; she had been alive for as long as the woman had been sick. Both characters remain unnamed yet are called "daughter." Both would have been considered unclean, yet Jesus came into direct contact with both.

Furthermore, there is the subject of faith. Jesus' response to the woman makes clear the importance of her faith—it is what Jesus attributes her healing to. But there is also the faith of Jairus for his daughter. Jesus urged him, "Just believe." When Jesus arrives at his home, He makes those who doubt in her healing leave. The gospels of both Matthew and Mark make clear that they were not allowed to be present when Jesus proceeded to raise her back to life. In other words, their lack of faith hindered the miraculous.

This happens more than once in Scripture. Jesus goes to an area where people doubt him, and the Bible says the miraculous just isn't welcomed. In the very next chapter of Mark's account, it says, "He could not do any miracles there, except lay hands on a few sick people and heal them. He was amazed at their lack of faith."

The book of Matthew goes on to connect miracles to faith, and not until after these accounts does Jesus send out the twelve on their own. These miracles are their blueprint, their example. Jesus knew His disciples needed to witness a demonstration before they were prepared to teach and heal themselves.

The disciples believed in God; they believed in Yahweh. They worshiped at the temple, and though it isn't explicitly stated in Scripture, the general consensus of scholars is that they were all Jews. They would have grown up accustomed to following God. What Jesus did looked radically different than what they knew or anticipated.

Much like we saw with Rahab, an unexpected ally to God's people, or Ruth the Moabite being in the direct lineage of the Messiah, or the Israelite's victory over Sisera being credited to a woman, God continuously uses the most unlikely in His plans. Jesus knows that His ministry is likewise not what they expected, and He is therefore guiding them, teaching them that His presence in their lives requires faith, not works.

In John 14:1, Jesus gives a farewell speech. It's the Last Supper, and He knows their faith is about to be tested beyond anything they've seen or experienced yet. He says to them, "You believe in God, believe also in me." In other words, He is saying, "We're one—God and Jesus are one—so you can have faith."

Now, it's easy to look at these accounts and start to equate having faith with some kind of magic formula to solve all our problems. Sometimes the answer, no matter how great our faith, is still no.

In the book of Daniel is the infamous story of Shadrach, Meshach, and Abednego and the fiery furnace. When King Nebuchadnezzar tries to force his religion onto the three Israelites, they refuse. In their response they showcase what real faith means: pledging allegiance with no guarantee you'll get the answer you want. Before being cast into the fiery furnace, Shadrach, Meshach, and Abednego declare to King Nebuchadnezzar that although God is certainly able to rescue them, "Even if He does not, O king, you can be sure that we still will not serve your gods and we will not worship the golden statue you erected."

In their powerful statement of faith—"Even if He does not"—they don't say, "if He can't." These three aren't giving God a caveat or some kind of loophole "just in case." They're making a declaration of faith, of how absolutely certain they are of what they can't see, knowing that sometimes our plan isn't His.

Sometimes, on this side of eternity, healing doesn't happen. Jesus didn't come to earth to perform miracles. He can, and still does, but we have a tendency to fixate on the miracle and miss the message. Look at what He says in John 20.

He appears to His disciples after His resurrection, but Thomas is struggling to believe. Jesus tells him to touch his wounds and put his hand in Jesus' side where the Roman soldiers had pierced him. He knows that Thomas needs the tangible, touchable proof that we as humans instinctively crave. We want physical, quantifiable facts.

When Thomas reaches out and feels the scars, he finally believes, but check out Jesus' response: "Because you have seen me, you have believed; blessed are those who have not seen and yet have believed."

Brothers and sisters, that's us! We're the ones who haven't seen Jesus in the flesh, yet we have believed. In Hebrews, Paul defines faith as "the assurance of things hoped for, the conviction of things not seen." Miracles happen in a moment, but faith is forever. A miracle gets you through a hard time in this life, and faith ensures our eternity in the next.

Reflection

1. Luke was on a mission when he wrote his gospel account. A Roman official named Theophilus wanted proof of Jesus' divinity, and miracles were the tool that Luke chose.

2. The word daughter, in Greek, translates as "daughter of God" and "acceptable to God, rejoicing in God's peculiar care and protection."

3. What do you find most hinders your faith? What distractions make it hard to believe in the supernatural?

4. Consider how the visible aspect of fulfilling the law could actually hinder a person's faith.

5. John 3:16 is perhaps the most well-known verse in the Bible. What does it say was Jesus' purpose in coming to earth?

6. Read Luke 4:42. Why does Jesus say He has come to earth?

7. If miracles weren't Jesus' reason for coming to earth, why did He perform them?

About the Author

Writing professionally for nearly twenty years, Heather Preston, founder of Basileia Writing, is known for bringing a unique lens to the craft. With a Master of Arts in Theological Studies, she enjoys consulting for local churches and pastors, as well as academic collaborations. Her podcast delves into some of the theological questions she is most frequently asked by followers. When not writing, Heather most enjoys quality time with her husband and three kids.

To contact Heather regarding speaking engagements or other inquiries, email: heather@basileiawriting.com. Or go to her podcast entitled *Scripts on Scripture*.